WORD SEARCH FOR KIDS!

100 puzzles!

DJAPE

THIS IS

_____'s

(your name)

BOOK :)

First edition: May 2014

ISBN 978-1-49966-952-7

Word Search for KIDS!

Welcome, kids! This book is for you! And it's fun! :) It's full of Word Search puzzles. Well, what are they? Very simple! They contain a list of words that you must find in the grid.

A word can be found in the grid in one of the following 8 directions:

→	Horizontal Left to right	←	Horizontal Right to left
↓	Vertical Top to bottom	↑	Vertical Bottom to top
↘	Diagonal Top-left to bottom-right	↖	Diagonal bottom-right to top-left
↗	Diagonal Bottom-left to top-right	↙	Diagonal Top-right to bottom-left

And that's all! Just be patient and persistent, look for the whole string of characters and once you find the whole word, either cross it out or mark it in some way as "found".

Once you've found all words in a puzzle, some letters in the grid will not belong to any words. Circle them and write them down below the grid in the space provided. See what happens! :)

At the end of the book there are some surprises for you! What they are is for your elders to find out and help you out with. If you like them, you can find more such puzzles in my **"Puzzles for Kids" book**.

Enough talking! Start finding those letters and words! :)

KIDS, ENJOY! :)

DJAPE

1. KIDS' WORDS

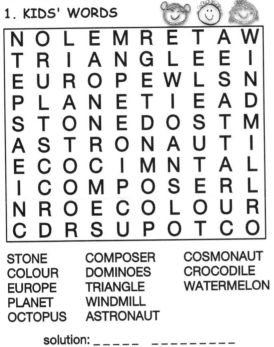

```
N O L E M R E T A W
T R I A N G L E E I
E U R O P E W L S N
P L A N E T I E A D
S T O N E D O S T M
A S T R O N A U T I
E C O C I M N T A L
I C O M P O S E R L
N R O E C O L O U R
C D R S U P O T C O
```

STONE   COMPOSER   COSMONAUT
COLOUR   DOMINOES   CROCODILE
EUROPE   TRIANGLE   WATERMELON
PLANET   WINDMILL
OCTOPUS   ASTRONAUT

solution: _ _ _ _ _ _ _ _ _ _ _ _ _ _

2. CARS

```
G O S H C A B Y A M R D
A L P I N E L I G I E R
G I H C N A I B O T U A
P O D M O G I R R S S L
S A L N A T E A E U T L
A K G I T N B R H B A A
K E E A A A M O T I H N
R B G U N T W B S S I C
A U L T L I H U E H A I
B T E S U B A R U I D A
```

BMW   LANCIA   MAYBACH
MAN   LIGIER   RENAULT
ROBUR   PAGANI   TRABANT
ALLARD   SINGER   DAIHATSU
ALPINE   SUBARU   MITSUBISHI
BARKAS   BUGATTI   AUTOBIANCHI
ESTHER   GOLIATH

solution: _ _ _ _ _ _ _ _ _ _ _ _

10. KIDS' WORDS

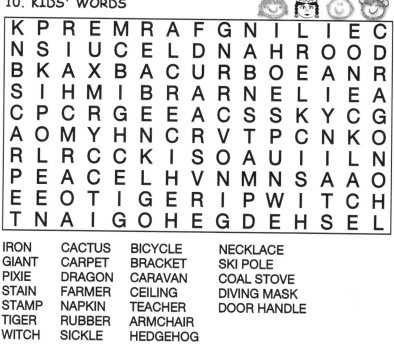

```
K P R E M R A F G N I L I E C
N S I U C E L D N A H R O O D
B K A X B A C U R B O E A N R
S I H M I B R A R N E L I E A
C P C R G E E A C S S K Y C G
A O M Y H N C R V T P C N K O
R L R C C K I S O A U I I L N
P E A C E L H V N M N S A A O
E E O T I G E R I P W I T C H
T N A I G O H E G D E H S E L
```

IRON	CACTUS	BICYCLE	NECKLACE
GIANT	CARPET	BRACKET	SKI POLE
PIXIE	DRAGON	CARAVAN	COAL STOVE
STAIN	FARMER	CEILING	DIVING MASK
STAMP	NAPKIN	TEACHER	DOOR HANDLE
TIGER	RUBBER	ARMCHAIR	
WITCH	SICKLE	HEDGEHOG	

solution: _ _ _ _ _ _ _   _ _ _ _ _ _

11. FLOWERS

```
M W A X F L O W E R F Y
U O T E N N O B E U L B
I L D E N V A G L I O D
L L R O I I N I L B R I
L A S O L I D A S T E R
I M L H G O L U M O T R
R E A K F L O R I S T C
T D N F A I L L E M A C
H I A C I N O R E V I D
P D E G N A R O K C O M
```

DAHLIA	CAMELLIA	CALLA LILY
FLORET	DAFFODIL	SOLIDASTER
MALLOW	TRILLIUM	WAX FLOWER
VIOLET	VERONICA	MOCK ORANGE
FLORIST	BLUEBONNET	PINK GINGER

solution: _ _ _ _ _ _ _ _ _ _   _ _ _ _ _ _

12. KIDS' WORDS

```
N I A T N U O F C N R H R L E
J T G I S N E T T L E I E T N
A O Y E L B A T E G E V V M A
N N M A R K E T P L A C E E V
U K N U R T O W I N T E R L R
A P A E D I A T R I C I A N E
R R S A T E L L I T E D I S H
Y S T A T U E H T U O Y E P T
E A I S D V E K C O Q R I L A
U A C H O P S T I C K S V U E
L T S H I E H C A T S U O M W
B A S K E T B A L L E O M M N
```

BLUE	KNOT	MOUSTACHE
KITE	NETTLE	VEGETABLE
PLUM	SHOVEL	BASKETBALL
MOVIE	STATUE	CHOPSTICKS
NAVEL	WINTER	MARKETPLACE
RIVER	JANUARY	GYMNASTICS
TRUNK	FEBRUARY	WEATHER VANE
YOUTH	FOUNTAIN	PAEDIATRICIAN
ELEVEN	MOSQUITO	SATELLITE DISH

solution: _ _ _ _ _ _ _ _ _   _ _ _ _ _ _ _ _ _ _

13. MATH

```
E L G N A E S U T B O C
E M I R P T A M R E F O
N A H T S S E L P N A O
O I N D E X A I O S D R
R E T A E R G G S O D D
R E F L E X A N G L E I
N D I M S T Y T T Q N N
R I U B C U T A I I D A
O N N O C U B E R O O T
S U B T R A C T I O N E
```

RAY	NUMERAL	COORDINATE
INDEX	OCTAGON	SUBTRACTION
ADDEND	CUBE ROOT	FERMAT PRIME
Q.E.D.	ITERATION	OBTUSE ANGLE
GREATER	LESS THAN	REFLEX ANGLE

solution: _ _ _ _ _ _ _   _ _ _ _ _ _ _ _ _ _ _

14. KIDS' WORDS

```
E H M F P M E S C D
S V O O I U L A O C
A T I O O I P P P I
I N A T P N A P P Y
R E T P O C I L E H
P E E R L M C E R T
O R A I B E O I N T
R E N N I W R C O E
T T H T A P T O O F
E C A L P E R I F L
```

HOOP	PUPPET	FIREPLACE
MOON	WINNER	FOOTPRINT
ROOT	AIRPORT	HELICOPTER
APPLE	SLIPPER	LOCOMOTIVE
NAPPY	STAPLER	
COPPER	FOOTPATH	

solution: _ _ _ _ _ _ _ _   _ _ _ _ _ _ _

15. DOGS

```
D B U L L T E R R I E R K A M
E N L S L E C H O W C H O W E
D N U O H H O A R A H P M U R
I E A O O I A N N C A N O Z S
T H I D H D B S B E A F N T F
O C R L T R H A A E C D D H S
H W I R L A E O I A R O O I E
T O E R R O E T U N P G R H I
E L G A E B C R T N U S E S E
C A N A A N D O G O D R O R O
```

BEAGLE	SHIBA INU	LHASA APSO
COLLIE	BLOODHOUND	OTTERHOUND
LOWCHEN	CANAAN DOG	BULL TERRIER
KOMONDOR	CANE CORSO	PHARAOH HOUND
SHIH TZU	GREAT DANE	
CHOW CHOW	LEONBERGER	

solution: _ _ _ _ _ _ _ _   _ _ _ _ _ _ _ _ _ _ _ _ _ _   _ _ _ _ _ _ _

16. KIDS' WORDS

```
S C H O E O H S O M
X L T T N C N A I E
C Y E S E O R C T N
O T L I W M R E O O
M R E O S O P T P H
P O P A P L R L A P
A F H H A H A D E O
S C O R P I O N T X
S N N O E K E N D A
E R E Y R R O L E S
```

ROOF	TEAPOT	SAXOPHONE
SHOE	TEMPLE	TELEPHONE
SNOW	COMPASS	XYLOPHONE
FORTY	ISLAND	MICROPHONE
LORRY	SCORPION	
SWORD	NEWSPAPER	

solution: _ _ _ _ _ _   _ _ _ _ _ _ _ _ _

17. CATS

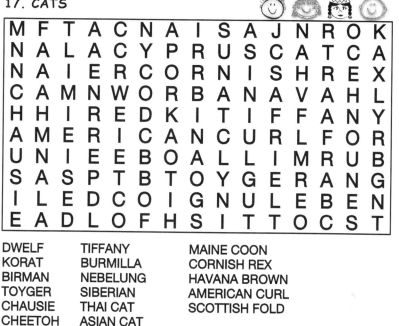

```
M F T A C N A I S A J N R O K
N A L A C Y P R U S C A T C A
N A I E R C O R N I S H R E X
C A M N W O R B A N A V A H L
H H I R E D K I T I F F A N Y
A M E R I C A N C U R L F O R
U N I E E B O A L L I M R U B
S A S P T B T O Y G E R A N G
I L E D C O I G N U L E B E N
E A D L O F H S I T T O C S T
```

DWELF	TIFFANY	MAINE COON
KORAT	BURMILLA	CORNISH REX
BIRMAN	NEBELUNG	HAVANA BROWN
TOYGER	SIBERIAN	AMERICAN CURL
CHAUSIE	THAI CAT	SCOTTISH FOLD
CHEETOH	ASIAN CAT	
KORN JA	CYPRUS CAT	

solution: _ _ _ _ _ _ _ _ _ _   _ _ _ _ _ _ _ _   _ _ _

18. KIDS' WORDS

```
A R E B O T C O F D
D A T T U S G N I W
O R N H U T T C D E
G E A I R N T O O F
A P C G K I L O V L
P A E R O P L A N E
H P O N H N M R W N
I T A I S T F U M N
S R N S T O O L P U
Y A S T W E N T Y T
```

FOOT	PAGODA	PUMPKIN
WING	TUNNEL	BUTTON
PAPER	TWENTY	AEROPLANE
STOOL	WALNUT	DRAGONFLY
STORK	DOLPHIN	DICTIONARY
STOVE	OCTOBER	

solution: _ _ _ _ _ _   _ _ _ _ _ _ _ _ _

- 13 -

19. FISH

```
P H Y T E N P O U N D E R U M
I O E U Y E L L O W T A N G H
N B L A C K S W A L L O W E R
T U L L N U D O T T Y B A C K
A H O E Y R M U N U Y K U N U
N C W K U F S Q U A W F I S H
O O T M H S I F M U P A I R P
P U A L U M P S U C K E R S A
P R I C K L Y S H A R K P U H
A A L M A N O F W A R F I S H
```

CHUB
DRUM
POWEN
PINTANO
DOTTYBACK
PLATYFISH

POLLYFISH
SQUAWFISH
LUMPSUCKER
TENPOUNDER
YELLOWTAIL
PRIAPUMFISH

YELLOW TANG
PRICKLY SHARK
BLACK SWALLOWER
MAN-OF-WAR FISH

solution: _ _ _ _ _ _ _ _ - _ _ _ _ _ _ _ _ - _ _ _ _ ' _

20. KIDS' WORDS

```
W T N W O L C A S S
H R E W O M N W A L
I U M N O N G P N E
C O O O G R H M D N
O L N V R A C O R N
U F G E R N M A F U
N E T M V K I L C F
T N A B F O O N O H
R C N E B O L G G I
Y E K R R C X G N E
```

FOG
FOX
COOK
SAND
TANK
ACORN
CLOWN

CROWN
FENCE
FLOOR
FLOUR
GLOBE
GLOVE
GNOME

FUNNEL
MAGNET
COUNTRY
MORNING
NOVEMBER
PHARMACY
LAWNMOWER

solution: _ _ _ _ _ _ _ _ _ _ _ _ _ _

21. VOCABULARY

```
E S Y T I V I T C A P S
M L U L N T R E V B U S
A S B O E E O H I O S T
N O U A R T V V R L A A
I L A R L O U O I E L T
P V V N V U V L L P V U
U E E T D I C I O C A A
L N L H B I V L N S G R
A T V R R R V E A R E Y
T N E M E V E I H C A R
E H T S O U N E V E N C
P Y E L B A U L A V N I
```

PIVOT   SOLVENT   RESOLUTELY
VIVID   SUBVERT   ACHIEVEMENT
CLOVEN   SURVIVE   CARNIVOROUS
UNEVEN   ACTIVITY   HERBIVOROUS
VELVET   STATUARY   INCALCULABLE
SALVAGE   INVALUABLE
SERVILE   MANIPULATE

solution: _ _ _ _ _ _ _ _ _ _ _ _

22. KIDS' WORDS

```
T A E B O R D R A W
S R E H T O R B B L
R F C A R T O O N R
A Y A E T E W N U E
M A T C H A S A N T
N D E N T I S T O T
N S E C I O O D R U
S E H S N U R S E B
B U S I K U C Y H A
T T D T M O T T O B
```

DESK   NURSE   DENTIST
DRUM   WATCH   FACTORY
MARS   BOTTOM   TUESDAY
NEST   BUTTER   DINOSAUR
HERON   BROTHER   WARDROBE
MATCH   CARTOON   CROSSWORD

solution: _ _ _ _ _ _ _ _ _ _ _ _ _ _

23. FLOWERS

```
D E L P H I N I U M P N
R A L L I U M D M H A A
A E I R E G N I G D E R
J N W S L A S H P E F C
A N N O E T C C H O U I
S A Z A L E A R L P J S
M S I E C F R O O S I S
I O T R C H Y F X C M U
N O A I S K N A B I U S
E D L O G I R A M D M S
```

CANNA   BANKSIA   MISTLETOE
PHLOX   FREESIA   NARCISSUS
ALLIUM   JASMINE   DELPHINIUM
AZALEA   FUJI MUM   RED GINGER
CROCUS   MARIGOLD
ORCHID   MAYFLOWER

solution: _ _ _ _ _ _ _ _ _ _ _ _ _ _ _ _ _

24. KIDS' WORDS

```
E F Y E N R U O J H
B N T O O T H M O C
U I I Y O J U E N I
G W R G N I N N U R
N O I D R O C C A T
I O I A E E P C O S
R D U R T U B R L O
R Q I R F R R U A A
A F R O A A A R A H
E A I W C L W C A Y
```

HOE	WOOD	OSTRICH
JOY	ARROW	RUNNING
BIRD	TOOTH	AQUARIUM
CART	CARROT	ACCORDION
FIRE	EARRING	AFTERNOON
HARP	JOURNEY	AUBERGINE

solution: _ _ _ _ _ _ _ _ _   _ _ _ _ _ _ _

25. ANIMALS

```
B U L L S N A K E T A M
T E R A T O S A U R U S
F S U R U A S O R B A F
E R B G N O R U T N I B
R I U C I T U O G A A N
P I R I E O H S W O N S
T B G K T U R T L E U L
L T A E R B R L O U S E
B L U E S H A R K I G E
S U R U A S O T A P A R
```

GRUB	SNOWSHOE	LAKE TROUT
SLUG	BINTURONG	APATOSAURUS
LOUSE	FRUIT BAT	FABROSAURUS
AGOUTI	BLUE SHARK	TERATOSAURUS
TURTLE	BULL SNAKE	

solution: _ _ _ _ _ _ _ _   _ _ _   _ _ _ _   _ _ _ _ _ _ _

26. KIDS' WORDS

```
N U S M O O R D E B F R C P B
I I E L T S E P E A R O H H R
G R L E T O H S M O K E A E U
H E E O M W T U K A W T M A S
T W N V D W O R N Y R E P S H
C O U S I N M G I D R M I A C
A L J S T E A K G H R A O N R
P F H P O R C M H O S E N T U
R E O L O P R E T A W T D A H
S K E O M O T O R B O A T R C
```

SUN	CANARY	PESTLE	PHEASANT
TWO	CHURCH	BEDROOM	RECEIVER
CROP	COUSIN	HUNDRED	MOTOR BOAT
JUNE	FLOWER	T-SHIRT	WATER POLO
BRUSH	KNIGHT	CHAMPION	BEST WISHES
HOTEL	MARMOT	KANGAROO	
SMOKE	METEOR	MANDOLIN	
STEAK	MOTHER	NIGHTCAP	

solution: _ _ _ _   _ _ _ _ _ _

27. MATH

```
T T S U B T R A H E N D
Y C O O R D I N A T E S
V R U O P E R A T I O N
A S A D R D B E I A S T
R I R N O E I M H B U T
I N I V I R R C U V E P
A E A R O B P A P N E R
B L H T D N A S U O H T
L A R E T A L I U Q E T
E W Y S E L E C S O S I
```

MEAN	PRODUCT	SUBTRAHEND
OVAL	SINE LAW	THOUSANDTH
CHAOS	VARIABLE	EQUILATERAL
BINARY	ISOSCELES	SQUARE ROOT
NUMBER	OPERATION	Y-COORDINATE

solution: _ _ _ _ _ _ _ _ _ _ _ _   _ _ _ _ _ _ _ _

28. TOUGH WORDS

```
D L N E T A L U M I T S
E I C A C T U A R Y U C
T C A A I S C O N O I N
A E M L P R E T R T O E
M N B M E I U E E I A P
I T U P O C T H T N R E
T I S A N S T U T H E N
L O H O O A L I L R E U
U U U P P O C S C A A R
N S E M S B R E V I T Y
E R Y B E S T R E W A E
P S A S E C L U S I O N
```

ANTIC   BREVITY   LICENTIOUS
AMBUSH   ARTHURIAN   PENULTIMATE
PENURY   SECLUSION   SYMPATHETIC
SEETHE   STIMULATE   DIALECTICIAN
ACTUARY   ABSOLUTION   PREPOSTEROUS
BESTREW   CAPITULATE

solution: _ _ _ _ _ _ _ _ _ _ _ _ _ _ _ _

29. FRUITS

```
B L O O D O R A N G E S
A A I N D I A N F I G P
C N M L A P L I O P O I
U Z A B L S I N Y A O G
P O B M A Y H O N C B E
A N O K E R P I Y E M O
R E L O R R E I P R A N
I S O A N E G L L O G P
Z I Z I P H U S L L V E
M U L P O C O C E A Y A
```

CHERRY   COCOPLUM   AMBARELLA
MABOLO   GAMBOOGE   INDIAN FIG
ACEROLA   LANZONES   LILLYPILLY
SHIPOVA   OIL PALM   PIGEON PEA
BACUPARI   ZIZIPHUS   BLOOD ORANGE

solution: _ _ _ _ _   _ _ _ _ _ _ - _ _ _ _ _ _

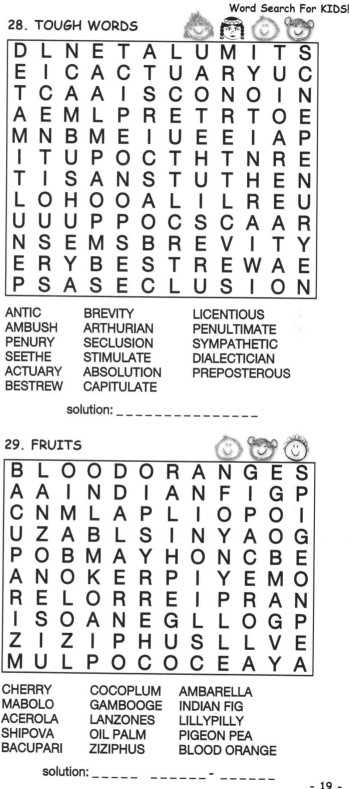

30. KIDS' WORDS

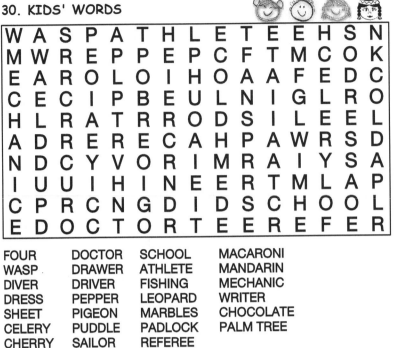

```
W A S P A T H L E T E E H S N
M W R E P P E P C F T M C O K
E A R O L O I H O A A F E D C
C E C I P B E U L N I G L R O
H L R A T R R O D S I L E E L
A D R E R E C A H P A W R S D
N D C Y V O R I M R A I Y S A
I U U I H I N E E R T M L A P
C P R C N G D I D S C H O O L
E D O C T O R T E E R E F E R
```

FOUR	DOCTOR	SCHOOL	MACARONI
WASP	DRAWER	ATHLETE	MANDARIN
DIVER	DRIVER	FISHING	MECHANIC
DRESS	PEPPER	LEOPARD	WRITER
SHEET	PIGEON	MARBLES	CHOCOLATE
CELERY	PUDDLE	PADLOCK	PALM TREE
CHERRY	SAILOR	REFEREE	

solution: _ _ _ _ _ _ _ _

31. FRUITS

```
G T I U R F N O R A H S
T I U R F R A T S O P A
Y R R E B E C I V R E S
Y R R E B W E D V E A K
C A R E M M O P R N C A
Y R R E B E L B M I H T
Y R R E B K C A L B O O
G N A R A M R A C S P N
L N A S A L U P G A U N
S H E E P B E R R Y I M
```

GAC	DEWBERRY	BLACKBERRY
ACAI	POMMERAC	SHEEPBERRY
PEACH	RUMBERRY	SERVICEBERRY
MARANG	SASKATOON	SHARON FRUIT
PULASAN	STARFRUIT	THIMBLEBERRY

solution: _ _ _ _ _ _ _ _ ' _ _ _ _ _

32. VOCABULARY

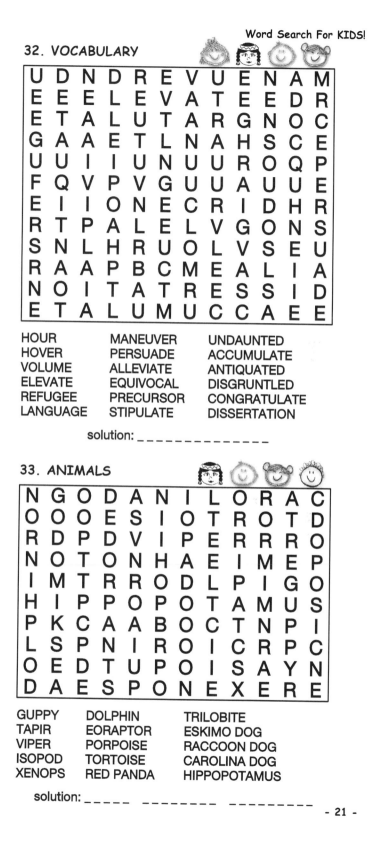

```
U D N D R E V U E N A M
E E E L E V A T E E D R
E T A L U T A R G N O C
G A A E T L N A H S C E
U U I I U N U U R O Q P
F Q V P V G U U A U U E
E I I O N E C R I D H R
R T P A L E L V G O N S
S N L H R U O L V S E U
R A A P B C M E A L I A
N O I T A T R E S S I D
E T A L U M U C C A E E
```

HOUR   MANEUVER   UNDAUNTED
HOVER   PERSUADE   ACCUMULATE
VOLUME   ALLEVIATE   ANTIQUATED
ELEVATE   EQUIVOCAL   DISGRUNTLED
REFUGEE   PRECURSOR   CONGRATULATE
LANGUAGE   STIPULATE   DISSERTATION

solution: _ _ _ _ _ _ _ _ _ _ _ _ _ _

33. ANIMALS

```
N G O D A N I L O R A C
O O O E S I O T R O T D
R D P D V I P E R R R O
N O T O N H A E I M E P
I M T R R O D L P I G O
H I P P O P O T A M U S
P K C A A B O C T N P I
L S P N I R O I C R P C
O E D T U P O I S A Y N
D A E S P O N E X E R E
```

GUPPY   DOLPHIN   TRILOBITE
TAPIR   EORAPTOR   ESKIMO DOG
VIPER   PORPOISE   RACCOON DOG
ISOPOD   TORTOISE   CAROLINA DOG
XENOPS   RED PANDA   HIPPOPOTAMUS

solution: _ _ _ _ _   _ _ _ _ _ _ _ _   _ _ _ _ _ _ _ _

34. KIDS' WORDS

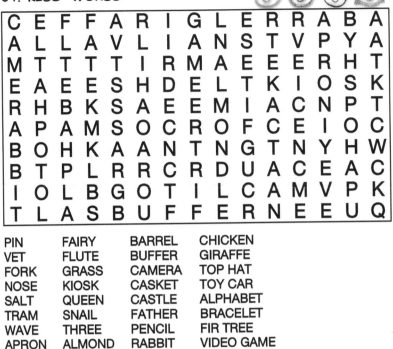

```
C E F F A R I G L E R R A B A
A L L A V L I A N S T V P Y A
M T T T T I R M A E E R H A T
E A E E S H D E L T K I O S K
R H B K S A E E M I A C N P T
A P A M S O C R O F C E I O C
B O H K A A N T N G T N Y H W
B T P L R R C R D U A C E A C
I O L B G O T I L C A M V P K
T L A S B U F F E R N E E U Q
```

PIN	FAIRY	BARREL	CHICKEN
VET	FLUTE	BUFFER	GIRAFFE
FORK	GRASS	CAMERA	TOP HAT
NOSE	KIOSK	CASKET	TOY CAR
SALT	QUEEN	CASTLE	ALPHABET
TRAM	SNAIL	FATHER	BRACELET
WAVE	THREE	PENCIL	FIR TREE
APRON	ALMOND	RABBIT	VIDEO GAME

solution: _ _ _ _ _   _ _ _ _ _

35. FRUITS

```
R Y R R E H C K C A L B
Y E B R E A D N U T R I
A R M M W E R I C A I L
Y R R E H C H S U R B B
N R S E D O U B A H E E
E H D R B O A S P B R R
J A M B U L C E R R R R
M U L P D N U O R G Y Y
A Y A T I P O M C I T E
S E R V I C E T R E E Y
```

CAWESH	RIBERRY
DOUBAH	BILBERRY
JAMBUL	BREADNUT
PITAYA	MULBERRY
POMCITE	COCO-DE-MER

GROUND PLUM
BLACK CHERRY
BRUSH CHERRY
SERVICE TREE

solution: _ _ _ _ _ _ _ _   _ _ _   _ _ _ _ _ _ _ _

36. KIDS' WORDS

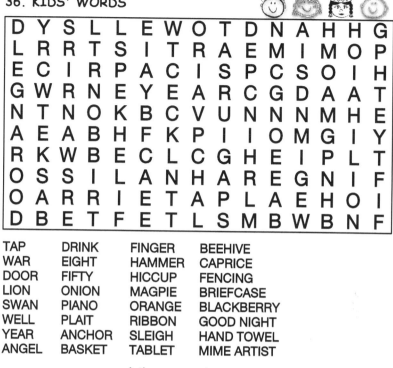

```
D Y S L L E W O T D N A H H G
L R R T S I T R A E M I M O P
E C I R P A C I S P C S O I H
G W R N E Y E A R C G D A A T
N T N O K B C V U N N M H E
A E A B H F K P I I O M G I Y
R K W B E C L C G H E I P L T
O S S I L A N H A R E G N I F
O A R R I E T A P L A E H O I
D B E T F E T L S M B W B N F
```

TAP	DRINK	FINGER	BEEHIVE
WAR	EIGHT	HAMMER	CAPRICE
DOOR	FIFTY	HICCUP	FENCING
LION	ONION	MAGPIE	BRIEFCASE
SWAN	PIANO	ORANGE	BLACKBERRY
WELL	PLAIT	RIBBON	GOOD NIGHT
YEAR	ANCHOR	SLEIGH	HAND TOWEL
ANGEL	BASKET	TABLET	MIME ARTIST

solution: _ _ _ _ ' _   _ _ _ _ _

37. ANIMALS

```
M N A O Z O T O R P W H
I I E S O O G N O M T E
Q S N O D O L A G E M P
D U N K L E O S T E U S
S O O R A G N A K D E R
O A P L A G O M O R P H
T T L P L E D D O L P H
S L A M I N A M R A F I
T E N R O H T O M M A M
N A N U T N I F E U L B
```

MINK	MAMMOTH	BLUEFIN TUNA
HIPPO	MONGOOSE	DUNKLEOSTEUS
QUOLL	LAGOMORPH	FARM ANIMALS
HORNET	MEGALODON	RED KANGAROO
SALMON	PROTOZOAN	

solution: _ _ _ _ _ -   _ _ _ _ _ _ _   _ _ _ _ _ _ _

38. CARS

```
G W A R T B U R G J M S
E G R J E N A J O R T C
Y R E O T R E W B A A S
D E E S M A E B N U S P
T B L S G T I D M E E I
R M B E T I A F N U R S
A U O C S R N O G A X E
M H N A D L S E C B W A
S O C R A M O S O G P T
G I N E T T A W E K N Z
```

MDI	EXAGON	STANDARD
PGO	HUMBER	WANDERER
FIAT	JOWETT	WARTBURG
SAAB	MARCOS	WOLSELEY
SEAT	TROJAN	JOSSE CAR
NOBLE	GINETTA	KOENIGSEGG
SMART	PEUGEOT	
ASCARI	SUNBEAM	

solution: _ _ _ _ _ _ _ _ - _ _ _ _

39. COMPOUND WORDS

```
H O M E W O R K S F B E M E I
O W E L T E R W E I G H T B E
M A A E Z P R R L N O O M V L
E Y D T Z O R L I N R O E A O
W W O U U Y Y Y E W C R D N H
A A W P B C A Y R Y Y R B Y
R R L O A S M E E B B U Y F B
D D A N S O D N O U S W E S B
S T R A O N O D G H A I O N U
A L K N U H Y A W Y E L L A C
```

ABUZZ	WAYWARD	HOMEWORK	HONEYMOON
BYWAY	ALLEYWAY	CUBBYHOLE	MEADOWLARK
LETUP	ASSAYING	EVERYBODY	UNDERWROTE
ONRUSH	BILLYCAN	FERRYBOAT	WELTERWEIGHT
LADYBUG	HOMEWARD	HONEYCOMB	

solution: _ _ _ _ _ _ _ _ _ _ _ _ _ _ _ _

40. FISH

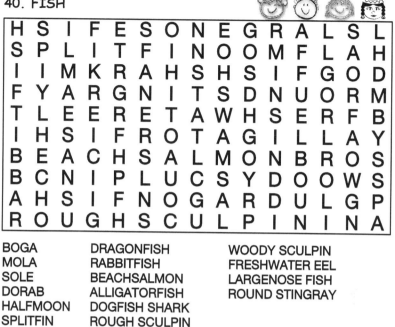

```
H S I F E S O N E G R A L S L
S P L I T F I N O O M F L A H
I I M K R A H S H S I F G O D
F Y A R G N I T S D N U O R M
T L E E R E T A W H S E R F B
I H S I F R O T A G I L L A Y
B E A C H S A L M O N B R O S
B C N I P L U C S Y D O O W S
A H S I F N O G A R D U L G P
R O U G H S C U L P I N I N A
```

BOGA	DRAGONFISH	WOODY SCULPIN
MOLA	RABBITFISH	FRESHWATER EEL
SOLE	BEACHSALMON	LARGENOSE FISH
DORAB	ALLIGATORFISH	ROUND STINGRAY
HALFMOON	DOGFISH SHARK	
SPLITFIN	ROUGH SCULPIN	

solution: _ _ _ _ _   _ _ _ _ _ _ _

41. FLOWERS

```
P W S I R T A I L T I N
A M O T I R T E I X H O
E V U L A A L C I S M G
T I L I F T K A A W I A
O B E L R S I N P E M R
R U O Y E U B C P E O D
P R M E S S H A E T S P
I N D S O S P T N P A A
R U A A R T S I N E G N
Y M U M D R A D N A T S
```

IXIA	PROTEA	VIBURNUM
LILY	LIATRIS	ANTHURIUM
ROSE	STATICE	SWEET PEA
SEPAL	TRITOMA	WOLFSBANE
MIMOSA	GENISTRA	SNAPDRAGON
MYRTLE	TICKSEED	STANDARD MUM

solution: _ _ _ _ _ _ _ _ _ _ _   _ _ _ _ _

42. VOCABULARY

```
P  E  F  F  E  C  T  U  A  T  E  Q
A  D  J  O  U  R  N  E  D  C  U  L
C  R  I  P  R  E  J  U  D  I  C  E
P  O  L  L  U  T  I  O  N  T  L  I
I  T  N  M  G  S  U  T  E  C  C  S
R  C  M  V  P  R  E  N  A  E  O  U
O  I  C  U  O  S  A  T  A  H  N  R
U  V  R  O  S  Y  P  D  E  T  V  E
E  N  R  E  N  E  N  S  U  R  E  L
T  O  N  I  C  V  D  O  I  A  R  Y
T  C  P  E  R  P  E  T  U  I  T  Y
E  N  R  U  T  E  R  Y  A  N  N  E
```

NOUN	CONVERT	POLLUTION
SPURN	CONVICT	PREJUDICE
CONVEY	GRADUATE	EFFECTUATE
CONVOY	ADJOURNED	PERPETUITY
ENSURE	FORTUNATE	RECEPTACLE
HECTIC	LEISURELY	QUINTESSENCE
RETURN	PIROUETTE	

solution: _ _ _ _ _   _ _ _ _ _ _ _ _

43. KIDS' WORDS

```
R E F R I G E R A T O R
E C O F F E E I I N J O
A T O G A F S U Y S E A
R N Y U M A R G O L I K
O T I U R F E P A R G C
H O U O I G R U S E H I
P A T W C R E I G I T R
M N I G H T G T N N Y B
A K E L G N U J T I O P
H A P P Y E A S T E R T
```

SEA	BRICK	JUNGLE
TEA	FAGOT	KILOGRAM
ASIA	NIGHT	COURGETTE
CHIN	COFFEE	GRAPEFRUIT
COIN	EIGHTY	KIWI FRUIT
HAIL	TONGUE	HAPPY EASTER
SIGN	AMPHORA	REFRIGERATOR

solution: _ _ _ _ _   _ _ _ _   _ _ _ _

44. ANIMALS

```
E S I O T R O T T R E S E D A
L L L R E T A K S D N O P D A
T B A V G O H T R A W R A E G
E R A H E R M I T C R A B R I
E E T A W N O J S E A S L U G
B O A R T E T U A T A R A T T
M L E R R I U Q S G N I Y L F
T Q U E T Z A L O E U R T U O
K R A H S L L U B B R A B V I
S E S R O H O R N S H A R K E
```

BARB	GROUSE	BLUE WHALE
HARE	JAGUAR	BULL SHARK
MOTH	QUETZAL	HORN SHARK
HORSE	TUATARA	HERMIT CRAB
TETRA	VULTURE	POND SKATER
BEAVER	WARTHOG	DESERT TORTOISE
BEETLE	SEA SLUG	FLYING SQUIRREL

solution: _ _ _ _ _ _ _   _ _ _ _ _   _ _ _ _ _ _ _ _

45. KIDS' WORDS

```
Q H C A M O T S U E
A T L I N E N R E S
D E C E M B E R T G
N N I G V B T C O O
A N D M E R H K D
P O N U M O N O N T
S B C O W M O I W O
A U L L R B W R N N
C I K C O G N I B G
K N A B R E M M U S
```

COW	BROOM	SUMMER
DOG	BROWN	EVENING
BANK	CHOIR	STOMACH
BOOK	CLOUD	CUCUMBER
SONG	LINEN	DECEMBER
TENT	PANDA	KILOMETRE
WIND	TONGS	
BINGO	BONNET	

solution: _ _ _ _ _ _ _ _ _ _ _ _ _

46. CARS

```
A A C S C H N I T Z E R
N A L P O E N O N I H G
B L S F T D R M O T O R
U O O R A C O R C I M I
S C A T E R H A M D M N
S I S N S S O T M U E N
I U R A V I K M R A L A
N F E R R A R I E A L L
G T O Y O T A B A O B L
R T I G U M P E R T N A
```

HSV	TOYOTA	CATERHAM
KIA	BRISTOL	DR MOTOR
AUDI	BUSSING	GRINNALL
HINO	FERRARI	MICROCAR
ABARTH	GUMPERT	ALFA ROMEO
DATSUN	HOMMELL	AC SCHNITZER
MORRIS	NEOPLAN	

solution: _ _ _ _ _ _ _ _ _ _ _

47. KIDS' WORDS

```
R  E  G  L  A  S  S  E  S  E
M  W  C  D  E  S  S  E  R  T
R  O  H  V  A  S  E  T  R  S
A  T  T  I  C  D  S  B  O  A
F  L  E  H  S  K  O  O  B  P
Y  A  D  R  U  T  A  S  N  H
T  H  I  R  T  Y  L  O  O  T
R  E  R  L  Y  T  T  E  J  O
A  L  E  R  R  I  U  Q  S  O
P  L  I  R  P  A  R  R  O  T
```

POT	PARTY	WHISTLE
FARM	BOTTLE	SATURDAY
TOOL	LESSON	SQUIRREL
VASE	PARROT	BOOKSHELF
APRIL	THIRTY	TOOTHPASTE
ATTIC	DESSERT	
JETTY	GLASSES	

solution: _ _ _ _ _ _ _ _

48. FISH

```
L  A  R  G  E  E  Y  E  B  R  E  A  M  H  T
B  O  M  B  A  Y  D  U  C  K  Y  S  S  H  E
W  A  S  U  E  C  K  O  E  U  R  I  O  M  N
O  E  N  P  F  U  L  T  C  H  F  R  A  R  U
L  R  E  A  I  D  N  I  F  Y  N  I  P  S  I
O  E  M  V  W  N  L  E  E  Y  A  R  O  M  S
U  V  O  I  E  O  Y  K  H  R  Y  R  U  A  S
V  L  F  E  L  R  R  E  G  N  O  W  R  O  M
A  E  D  C  A  U  A  A  E  A  T  S  C  U  P
R  E  G  I  T  D  N  A  S  L  F  I  S  H  M
```

AYU	ALEWIFE	MURRAY COD
SCUP	AROWANA	SAND TIGER
ELVER	MORWONG	THORNYHEAD
SAURY	OLDWIFE	TURKEYFISH
LOUVAR	SPINYFIN	BOMBAY DUCK
TENUIS	MORAY EEL	LARGE-EYE BREAM
WEEVER	SPINY EEL	

solution: _ _ _ _ _ _ _ _ _ _ _ _ _ _ _ _ _ _ _ _ _ _ _ _ _ _

49. KIDS' WORDS

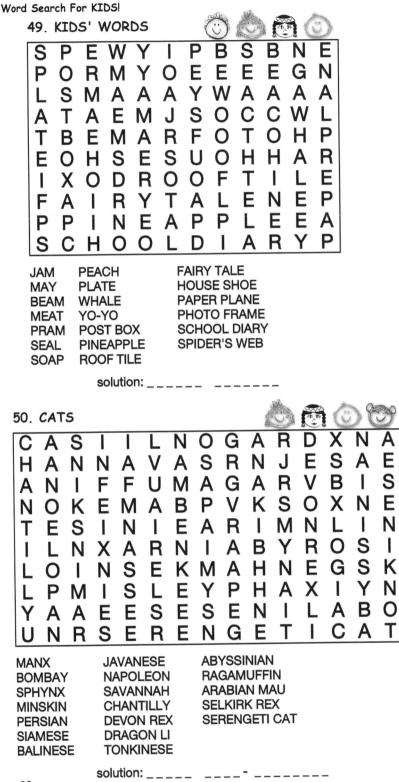

```
S P E W Y I P B S B N E
P O R M Y O E E E E G N
L S M A A A Y W A A A A
A T A E M J S O C C W L
T B E M A R F O T O H P
E O H S E S U O H H A R
I X O D R O O F T I L E
F A I R Y T A L E N E P
P P I N E A P P L E E A
S C H O O L D I A R Y P
```

JAM	PEACH	FAIRY TALE
MAY	PLATE	HOUSE SHOE
BEAM	WHALE	PAPER PLANE
MEAT	YO-YO	PHOTO FRAME
PRAM	POST BOX	SCHOOL DIARY
SEAL	PINEAPPLE	SPIDER'S WEB
SOAP	ROOF TILE	

solution: _ _ _ _ _ _   _ _ _ _ _ _ _

50. CATS

```
C A S I I L N O G A R D X N A
H A N N A V A S R N J E S A E
A N I F F U M A G A R V B I S
N O K E M A B P V K S O X N E
T E S I N I E A R I M N L I N
I L N X A R N I A B Y R O S I
L O I N S E K M A H N E G S K
L P M I S L E Y P H A X I Y N
Y A A E E S E S E N I L A B O
U N R S E R E N G E T I C A T
```

MANX	JAVANESE	ABYSSINIAN
BOMBAY	NAPOLEON	RAGAMUFFIN
SPHYNX	SAVANNAH	ARABIAN MAU
MINSKIN	CHANTILLY	SELKIRK REX
PERSIAN	DEVON REX	SERENGETI CAT
SIAMESE	DRAGON LI	
BALINESE	TONKINESE	

solution: _ _ _ _ _   _ _ _ _ - _ _ _ _ _ _ _ _

51. KIDS' WORDS

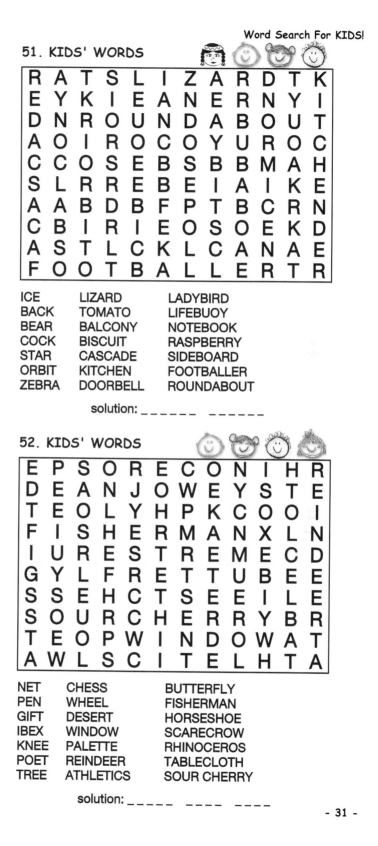

```
R A T S L I Z A R D T K
E Y K I E A N E R N Y I
D N R O U N D A B O U T
A O I R O C O Y U R O C
C C O S E B S B B M A H
S L R R E B E I A I K E
A A B D B F P T B C R N
C B I R I E O S O E K D
A S T L C K L C A N A E
F O O T B A L L E R T R
```

ICE	LIZARD	LADYBIRD
BACK	TOMATO	LIFEBUOY
BEAR	BALCONY	NOTEBOOK
COCK	BISCUIT	RASPBERRY
STAR	CASCADE	SIDEBOARD
ORBIT	KITCHEN	FOOTBALLER
ZEBRA	DOORBELL	ROUNDABOUT

solution: _ _ _ _ _ _   _ _ _ _ _ _

52. KIDS' WORDS

```
E P S O R E C O N I H R
D E A N J O W E Y S T E
T E O L Y H P K C O O I
F I S H E R M A N X L N
I U R E S T R E M E C D
G Y L F R E T T U B E E
S S E H C T S E E I L E
S O U R C H E R R Y B R
T E O P W I N D O W A T
A W L S C I T E L H T A
```

NET	CHESS	BUTTERFLY
PEN	WHEEL	FISHERMAN
GIFT	DESERT	HORSESHOE
IBEX	WINDOW	SCARECROW
KNEE	PALETTE	RHINOCEROS
POET	REINDEER	TABLECLOTH
TREE	ATHLETICS	SOUR CHERRY

solution: _ _ _ _ _   _ _ _ _   _ _ _ _

53. KIDS' WORDS

```
C Y P R E S S P R I Z E
I N D E X F I N G E R D
H T K C I H C B O F T A
A E T S W E E T I I I P
U N D E R G R O U N D S
M R O W H T R A E K H U
A L L A H G N I N I D G
I I R B A A A I P L L N
Z F R Y I N G P A N O U
E O L L U G A E S R N F
```

AIR	KNIFE	EARTHWORM
TEN	MAIZE	SPAGHETTI
IBIS	PRIZE	FRYING PAN
NAIL	SPADE	DINING-HALL
RAIN	SWEET	UNDERGROUND
SHIP	FUNGUS	INDEX FINGER
WHIP	SEAGULL	
CHICK	CYPRESS	

solution: _ _ _ - _ _ _ _ _ _ _ _ _ _

54. ANIMALS

```
N R G E N A S T E F R K
A A E U A O N N L L O A
I Y E D I W B O I L A N
T B R C N N W B N B U G
A A E D A A E U I M O A
M B G G R T M A B G G R
L H A D E O S A F E R O
A S N I M C T U L O Z O
D U A L O L K P R A W N
T B T I P A K O A C S L
```

ZEBU	NUMBAT	POMERANIAN
GECKO	TANAGER	SALAMANDER
OKAPI	BUSHBABY	GUINEA FOWL
PRAWN	KANGAROO	TUNDRA WOLF
ROBIN	DALMATIAN	
GIBBON	CRUSTACEAN	

solution: _ _ _ _ _ _ _ _ _ _ _ _ _ _ _ _ _ _ _ _ _

55. KIDS' WORDS

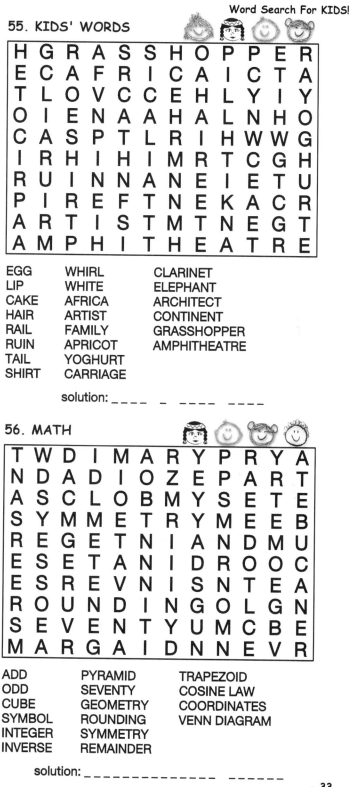

```
H G R A S S H O P P E R
E C A F R I C A I C T A
T L O V C C E H L Y I Y
O I E N A A H A L N H O
C A S P T L R I H W W G
I R H I H I M R T C G H
R U I N N A N E I E T U
P I R E F T N E K A C R
A R T I S T M T N E G T
A M P H I T H E A T R E
```

EGG · WHIRL · CLARINET
LIP · WHITE · ELEPHANT
CAKE · AFRICA · ARCHITECT
HAIR · ARTIST · CONTINENT
RAIL · FAMILY · GRASSHOPPER
RUIN · APRICOT · AMPHITHEATRE
TAIL · YOGHURT
SHIRT · CARRIAGE

solution: _ _ _ _   _   _ _ _ _   _ _ _ _

56. MATH

```
T W D I M A R Y P R Y A
N D A D I O Z E P A R T
A S C L O B M Y S E T E
S Y M M E T R Y M E E B
R E G E T N I A N D M U
E S E T A N I D R O O C
E S R E V N I S N T E A
R O U N D I N G O L G N
S E V E N T Y U M C B E
M A R G A I D N N E V R
```

ADD · PYRAMID · TRAPEZOID
ODD · SEVENTY · COSINE LAW
CUBE · GEOMETRY · COORDINATES
SYMBOL · ROUNDING · VENN DIAGRAM
INTEGER · SYMMETRY
INVERSE · REMAINDER

solution: _ _ _ _ _ _ _ _ _ _ _ _ _   _ _ _ _ _ _

57. KIDS' WORDS

```
Y A D N O M K C O S V A
C R G R A E N E U B U C
W O R R A B L E E H W A
K D E E R C R D D H M B
C P Y I B E T E N R C B
O C D L E W D S A A A A
R G E B R E A D O K C G
E E T U H C A R A P A E
W A T E R B O T T L E N
D R A O B E T A K S E R
```

BED   CHEEK   POSTCARD
BEER   OPERA   PARACHUTE
DEER   BRIDGE   SKATEBOARD
GREY   CANDLE   STRAWBERRY
ROCK   GARDEN   WHEELBARROW
SOCK   LADDER   WATER-BOTTLE
BREAD   MONDAY
BREAK   CABBAGE

solution: _ _ _ _ _ _   _ _ _ _ _ _ _

58. CHEMISTRY

```
T R S M M M M M M G X E
L M U E U U U U T O E N
A H U I A I I I I L N I
B E R I L B M L L D O D
O E R L R U O S E L N O
C F A E I O R R O B A I
O H T L R D H I G U O G
T M U I R U C T N I T N
M H G A D O L I N I U M
T M U I V E L E D N E M
```

TIN   IODINE   NOBELIUM
GOLD   OSMIUM   THALLIUM
XENON   GALLIUM   GADOLINIUM
CERIUM   TERBIUM   SEABORGIUM
COBALT   THORIUM   MENDELEVIUM
CURIUM   THULIUM
INDIUM   CHROMIUM

solution: _ _ _ _ _ _ _ _ _ _ _ _

59. KIDS' WORDS

```
R A G N R O C I N U T B
U I N U G D N A H R L A
B L C K F E M A F A C E
B L C E L E N E C K U R
I A O B C D L K F L O L
S B A I B R B E B T O I
H T L A D O E Y C C T V
C O G L A A K A K R E I
P O G R H S R T M S A W
S F D R O T A I D A R P
```

RAG   TABLE   FOOTBALL
SAW   PARCEL   RADIATOR
FACE   HANDBAG   SKY BLUE
LOCK   HANDGUN   ICE CREAM
NECK   RUBBISH   POLICEMAN
SACK   TRACTOR   BLACKBOARD
TEAR   UNICORN
RADIO   VOLCANO

solution: _ _ _ _ _ _ _   _ _ _ _ _ _

60. SPORTS

```
M A R T I A L A R T S L A O G
J A A P O W E R L I F T I N G
U G T B O D Y B U I L D I N G
J W R I D E A D L I F T I N G
I Z U R K H A N E H A I E I G
T R A C E G N I I K S E E P E
S H O O T I N G S P O R T L H
U H E N O N I E L O H T L I D
T E K C I R C R E T T I H O N
F T E R M I N O R L E A G U E
```

MAT   HOCKEY   HOLE-IN-ONE
TAG   SKIING   ICE SKATING
EPEE   CRICKET   BODYBUILDING
GOAL   JU-JITSU   MARTIAL ARTS
RACE   NO-HITTER   MINOR LEAGUE
RIDE   ZURKHANEH   POWERLIFTING
FIELD   DEADLIFTING   SHOOTING SPORT

solution: _ _ _ _ _ _ _ _ _ _ _ _

61. KIDS' WORDS

```
R  S  W  E  C  T  R  R  V  Y  E  A
Y  E  S  O  F  A  P  E  A  O  L  R
R  V  B  I  O  A  B  D  T  L  C  T
F  E  L  M  P  D  S  L  E  N  N  S
L  N  L  L  E  E  P  R  E  N  U  E
E  T  L  G  N  T  B  E  A  C  T  H
B  Y  D  D  G  M  P  E  C  F  A  C
E  U  E  Y  U  U  C  E  E  K  T  R
J  W  B  A  I  O  J  L  S  L  E  O
L  G  R  A  N  D  F  A  T  H  E  R
```

ON	JUDGE	UMBRELLA
PEA	OCEAN	CABLE CAR
RED	UNCLE	ORCHESTRA
LEFT	BELFRY	SEPTEMBER
LIFT	JUGGLER	WEDNESDAY
RAFT	PENGUIN	WOODPECKER
SAFE	SEVENTY	GRANDFATHER
SOFA	HUNTER	

solution: _ _ _ _ _ _ _ _ _ _

62. TOUGH WORDS

```
A  E  R  G  N  I  A  R  T  S  I  D  V  U  Y
S  X  E  A  R  O  I  T  R  E  V  A  I  F  V
U  C  M  R  A  L  I  M  R  T  P  N  I  S  I
O  U  O  R  P  O  A  S  M  O  T  R  B  U  S
I  R  N  O  I  T  A  N  R  E  T  S  N  O  C
R  S  S  T  D  J  C  I  R  E  R  X  I  R  O
A  I  I  E  U  A  Z  D  P  U  V  S  E  E  U
L  O  M  N  M  E  I  O  G  R  I  N  I  N  N
I  N  T  E  R  C  E  D  E  A  P  D  O  O  T
H  A  O  H  T  N  A  R  G  I  M  E  Y  C  N
```

AVER	ONEROUS	HILARIOUS
CAMEO	PETRIFY	IMMERSION
JUNTA	DISTRAIN	INTERCEDE
RAPID	EMIGRANT	INTERDICT
EXTORT	MISNOMER	VAPORIZER
DIURNAL	VISCOUNT	CONVERSION
GARROTE	EXCURSION	CONSTERNATION

solution: _ _ _ _ _ _ _ _ _ _ _ _ _ _

63. KIDS' WORDS

```
G H A M I L L I P E D E
G N I X O B G L E L O S
R O I P S N E S E I R U
I M P W I N K B L B M O
G M E R S I A Y U O I H
H I P T M L R C N M T T
T S E O L A K E K W O H
Y R F O R E H E A D R G
T E E R T S B E A R Y I
S P I H C A R N I V A L
```

OIL	RIGHT	STREET
TIE	SNACK	CARNIVAL
BALL	SWING	FOREHEAD
BELL	BOXING	DORMITORY
BELT	BUCKET	MILLIPEDE
LAKE	ESKIMO	PERSIMMON
RAKE	MOBILE	LIGHTHOUSE
CHIPS	SPRING	

solution: _ _ _ _ _   _ _ _   _ _ _ _

64. VOCABULARY

```
C O N D I T I O N E R D
D O M E S T I C A T E C
S R M J T O E P R T O Y
A K O E U A L E E M R R
N E I C S S L S M A A E
I T S T E N T U C T T F
T T T E T A N I C I A U
A L U D B I L U F L C G
R E R L T O S T I Y A E
Y V E Y S E E H A V O C
```

HAVOC	SANITARY	DEJECTEDLY
ACCUSE	SKITTISH	DETESTABLE
KETTLE	SOLITARY	CONDITIONER
REFUGE	SOLSTICE	DOMESTICATE
JUSTIFY	CALCULATE	
MOISTURE	COMMUNITY	

solution: _ _ _ _ _ _ _ _ _ _ _ _ _ _ _

65. KIDS' WORDS

```
E S E E H C A V S C H N
C P L L S U I T C A S E
I A L E C N C R E U U E
R C E E E Y A W N E R D
L E Z G F P C D F E B L
A C A F D R A R D R H E
D R G I A Y I I O P T B
N A S H E E P D O T O V
A F E K N S H E A D O R
S T A D I U M S Y Y T M
```

BEE	ACACIA	GAZELLE
KEY	CHEESE	STADIUM
BODY	FRIDAY	VINEGAR
POEM	FRIEND	SUITCASE
RICE	NEEDLE	MOTORCYCLE
SHEAF	SANDAL	SPACECRAFT
SHEEP	SPIDER	TOOTHBRUSH
SLEEP	SUNDAY	

solution: _ _ _ _ _ _ _ _ _ _ _

66. FLOWERS

```
F O X G L O V E H D R G
C H I C O R Y T A P E E
P R O T A L N N E A D R
L S U L O I D A L G N B
U P I N C E N E C U A E
M S H A L A V E N D E R
E I Y I Y S I A D R L A
R H O D O D E N D R O N
I N O I T A N R A C A D
A E G N A R D Y H O N G
```

DAISY	HYACINTH	DANDELION
CHICORY	LAVENDER	GLADIOLUS
GERBERA	OLEANDER	GOLDENROD
FOXGLOVE	PLUMERIA	HYDRANGEA
GARDENIA	CARNATION	RHODODENDRON

solution: _ _ _ _ _ _   _ _ _   _ _ _ _ _ _ _

67. KIDS' WORDS

```
M U E S U M W G M M O U
S T I C K P N O I N Y E
T N E P P I T T L E F U
H N O O L L A B K F G G
O P A C L O Y R L M N O
L I Y A N T U Y E E I G
L C W L E T Y L U J P A
Y E K N O M O O L G I N
E R I D O N K E Y A P Y
I N N G D R E H P E H S
```

FLY	IGLOO	NINETY
SKI	MELON	PIPING
HALL	PILOT	TURKEY
JULY	PYLON	BALLOON
MILK	STICK	CYCLING
WALL	DONKEY	SHEPHERD
WOLF	MONKEY	SYNAGOGUE
HOLLY	MUSEUM	FELT-TIP PEN

solution: _ _ _ _ _ _ _ _ _ _ _ _ _ _

68. ANIMALS

```
N S S G R I V E R T U R T L E
O Q I N A E E E P E S S A R W
G U H A M S T E R O H E M F O
A I G T R S T S E S S T O E R
R R F O B A Q I Y R G S N H R
D R Z O R U T I U O S N U A A
A E L S I F G F L A R O C M P
E L I D O C O R C F R A W D S
S E L W O D E R A E G N O L F
R O Y A L P E N G U I N I S H
```

FROG	POSSUM	FUR SEAL
TANG	WRASSE	SQUIRREL
CORAL	HAMSTER	SEA DRAGON
FOSSA	LOBSTER	RIVER TURTLE
SQUID	PANTHER	ROYAL PENGUIN
ZORSE	SPARROW	LONG-EARED OWL
OYSTER	TARSIER	DWARF CROCODILE

solution: _ _ _ _ _ _ _   _ _ _ _ _ _ _ _   _ _ _ _

69. KIDS' WORDS

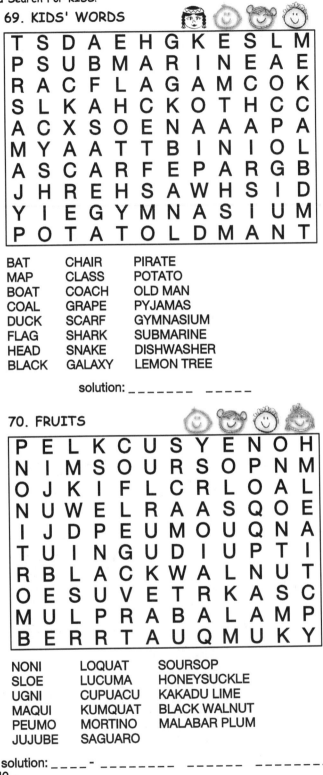

```
T S D A E H G K E S L M
P S U B M A R I N E A E
R A C F L A G A M C O K
S L K A H C K O T H C C
A C X S O E N A A A P A
M Y A A T B I N I O L
A S C A R F E P A R G B
J H R E H S A W H S I D
Y I E G Y M N A S I U M
P O T A T O L D M A N T
```

BAT	CHAIR	PIRATE
MAP	CLASS	POTATO
BOAT	COACH	OLD MAN
COAL	GRAPE	PYJAMAS
DUCK	SCARF	GYMNASIUM
FLAG	SHARK	SUBMARINE
HEAD	SNAKE	DISHWASHER
BLACK	GALAXY	LEMON TREE

solution: _ _ _ _ _ _ _   _ _ _ _ _

70. FRUITS

```
P E L K C U S Y E N O H
N I M S O U R S O P N M
O J K I F L C R L O A L
N U W E L R A A S Q O E
I J D P E U M O U Q N A
T U I N G U D I U P T I
R B L A C K W A L N U T
O E S U V E T R K A S C
M U L P R A B A L A M P
B E R R T A U Q M U K Y
```

NONI	LOQUAT	SOURSOP
SLOE	LUCUMA	HONEYSUCKLE
UGNI	CUPUACU	KAKADU LIME
MAQUI	KUMQUAT	BLACK WALNUT
PEUMO	MORTINO	MALABAR PLUM
JUJUBE	SAGUARO	

solution: _ _ _ _ - _ _ _ _ _ _ _ _   _ _ _ _ _ _   _ _ _ _ _ _ _ _ _

71. ANIMALS

```
S W A S P P E L T R U T A E S
L N O I L E L A H W N I F E S
A W O E A R W I G H E O E B O
V E R W T N O S I B X N I Y R
R A E B Y L Z Z I R G W A E T
E S D O P O R C U P I N E N A
S E W T U S W M S K U N K O B
U L O T S J E L L Y F I S H L
O E L E P H A N T S H R E W A
M A F R I G A T E B I R D N T
```

EMU	SKUNK	JELLYFISH
FOX	SERVAL	PORCUPINE
KIWI	WEASEL	SNOWY OWL
LION	EARWIG	TAWNY OWL
NEWT	PLATYPUS	SEA TURTLE
WASP	RED WOLF	FRIGATEBIRD
BISON	ALBATROSS	GRIZZLY BEAR
MOUSE	FIN WHALE	ELEPHANT SHREW
OTTER	HONEY BEE	

solution: _ _ _ _ _ _ _ _

72. TOUGH WORDS

```
I A L I E N O I T P M E E R P
M S E L B A R A P E R L C O M
M E O R N I S E L L M B F L O
I A I N D R N B T A I A L A M
N N E L O A A P E R S P I R E
E C N A M R O F N O C L P O N
N E L O E G O R A M O A P P T
T T R L I A O U N M U P A M O
P R O T R A C T S I N M N E U
N T N E R R U C E R T I T T S
```

ALIEN	AGRARIAN	SONOROUS	IMPALPABLE
BRINE	FLIPPANT	TEMPORAL	PREEMPTION
ENAMOR	IMMINENT	MOMENTOUS	CONFORMANCE
INROAD	MISCOUNT	RECURRENT	
SEANCE	PERSPIRE	REPARABLE	
IMMORAL	PROTRACT	TOLERABLE	

solution: _ _ _ _ _ _ _ _ _ _ _ _ _

73. TOUGH WORDS

```
B D I Y T E I R P O R P M I N
L R E E S N O I T P U R R O C
A I N S T A N T A N E O U S E
S D I R P E C G C D W O Y I L
P S U N L O N C C U N E S O L
H D E L B I T S U A H X E N I
E K O R R O N U R R E V O O P
M P I R D S R P A F S C P M S
E G A L L E O N C E R E I I I
M B I N N S R A Y D T E D K S
```

WEE	BARRING	ACCURSED
KILN	DEFRAUD	ELLIPSIS
SEER	GALLEON	BLASPHEME
POESY	INTRUDE	CORRUPTION
DESPOT	OVERRUN	IMPROPRIETY
INBORN	REDRESS	INEXHAUSTIBLE
KIMONO	SOPRANO	INSTANTANEOUS
POLLEN	ACCURACY	

solution: _ _ _ _ _ _ _ _ _ _ _ _ _ _

74. SPORTS

```
L L S H C O M P E T I T O R O
P L A Y I N G N I L T S E R W
O A A R P Y T D U G O U T T R
L B A B M C O D N O W K E A T
E S P U Y S K I J U M P I N G
V I H L L E W K H A E R V S P
A N C C A O L C L E E V O M E
U N U D R Y T L S W T T I M K
L E O H A I E F O R W A R D A
T T T T P T I R E V I U Q N G
```

GYM	PITCH	QUIVER	COMPETITOR
MVP	ROWER	FORWARD	PARALYMPIC
CLUB	TOUCH	PLAYING	POLE VAULT
DIVE	DUGOUT	THROWING	VOLLEYBALL
MITT	MALLET	TAEKWONDO	SKI JUMPING
MOVE	PLAYER	WRESTLING	TENNIS-BALL

solution: _ _ _ _ _   _ _ _ _ _   _ _ _ _ _   _ _ _ _ _ _ _

75. KIDS' WORDS

```
S S Q U A R E S S A L G
E N T R Y P H O N E E W
B A R B E R U O B R A H
H E I S M C M B I T F C
K J N D W B N M B A C H
Y L I L R E T A W E R A
T R A E H A A B D H A I
A N R H O R Z T A T N N
O G T G C D P I E R E O
C O E Y E B R O W R C L
```

HAT	CRANE	WIZARD
BEAN	GLASS	EYEBROW
COAT	HEART	HARBOUR
CRAB	JEANS	SWEATER
GOAT	TRAIN	THEATRE
LEAF	BAMBOO	WATER LILY
BEARD	BARBER	ENTRY PHONE
CHAIN	DANCER	
CHALK	SQUARE	

solution: _ _ _ _ _ _ _ _ _ _ _ _

76. MATH

```
N O I T C E S R E T N I
E C N E U Q E S N Y D T
E D I A M E T E R T N G
F T N E I C I F F E O C
I R E G E D O O G N R I
F F H A A R E N N I I R
T T A R M N A M G N G C
Y I G U L T R A E N I L
P O L Y H E D R O N N E
M A T H E M A T I C S E
```

PI	NINETY	SEQUENCE
FIFTY	ORIGIN	POLYHEDRON
CIRCLE	FORMULA	COEFFICIENT
EIGHTY	TANGENT	MATHEMATICS
LINEAR	DIAMETER	INTERSECTION
MEDIAN	GRADIENT	

solution: _ _ _ _ _ _ _ _ _ _ _ _ _ _ _

77. SPORTS

```
L O O P W I N D S U R F I N G
L L F G N I T A K S D E E P S
U B A S I N N E T T F O S L H
C A A B U C S D Z T U L A G O
S T F R Y W R E S T L E R R R
W O R H T E E R F U B A S E T
O N O W O R L D S E R I E S S
S I N N E T E L B A T F W O T
P E N T A T H L O N T I E L O
B A G N I T L U A V M L L R P
```

OUT	SCUBA	SOFT TENNIS
RUN	SCULL	VOLLEY BALL
BASE	VAULTING	WINDSURFING
LUTZ	WRESTLER	TABLE TENNIS
POOL	SHORTSTOP	WORLD SERIES
SWIM	FREE THROW	SPEED SKATING
BATON	PENTATHLON	
LOSER	WINDSURFER	

solution: _ _ _ _   _ _ _ _ _ _ _ _

78. COMPOUND WORDS

```
J O V E R P O W E R I N G U U
W O T N K S P U K C I P H F N
E P H N G C O W T D E O W A D
S V L N I N A M Y D N A H I E
T O E A N H I B E E O R A R R
W U N R Y Y O Y Y W U R T Y W
A T O L Y P C B L G H O N T O
R G L G I O E A S T G A O A R
D O H E A E N N K D U I T L L
M U N D E R D E V E L O P E D
```

INTO	WHATNOT	FAIRYTALE
ONTO	EVERYONE	MOLLYHAWK
OUTDO	HANDYMAN	PIGGYBACK
OUTGO	HONEYBEE	JOHNNYCAKE
PICKUP	OUTLYING	UNDERWORLD
RAGOUT	SOMEWHAT	OVERPOWERING
PLAYPEN	WESTWARD	UNDERDEVELOPED

solution: _ _ _ _ _ _ _ _ _ _ _ _ _ _

79. FRUITS

```
C O C N A L B O R O C C
A E T A K I H A K A L L
N I E M G N A Y R E H A
A E R N R Y G A M O F L
L W A T E R M E L O N A
R Y R R E B N O M L A S
O T W H O T I U H T E R
K E Y L I M E I O G U R
Y C A N T A L O U P E N
A B E T E L N U T N D E
```

YEW	YANGMEI	CANTALOUPE
HUITO	KEY LIME	CLEMENTINE
SALAL	BETEL NUT	WATERMELON
BIGNAY	CARAMBOLA	SALMONBERRY
KORLAN	KAHIKATEA	
NUTMEG	OROBLANCO	

solution: _ _ _ _ _ _   _ _   _ _ _   _ _ _   _ _ _ _ _ _

80. ANIMALS

```
D Z E H S J O B Y J R A
A I L E L A O R A R L N
C G N R E C C C R O O W
H I N O S K K H R O G D
S B U N S R W I I S Z T
H S U R U A S A R T L U
U H T S M B U E L E O R
N R S F L B I R D R Y N
D E R A G I R E G D U B
L W A R H T R A N E X S
```

BIRD	CHITON	XENARTHRA
DORY	WALRUS	BUDGERIGAR
HERON	MUSSELS	JACK RABBIT
LORIS	ROOSTER	JACK RUSSEL
SHREW	DINOSAUR	ULTRASAURUS
ZORRO	DACHSHUND	

solution: _ _ _ _ _   _ _ _ _ _ _ _ _   _ _ _ _ _ _ _ _ _

81. TOUGH WORDS

```
H  E  A  R  T  I  L  Y  T  R  D  C
R  R  L  A  R  U  E  N  O  N  O  S
E  U  E  B  M  I  A  T  E  M  I  E
C  T  C  O  I  T  A  C  M  R  N  L
O  R  E  N  I  T  S  I  R  P  A  I
N  U  N  R  C  E  S  I  S  I  U  T
S  N  R  E  D  S  T  E  T  C  S  C
T  I  P  N  A  A  V  A  G  I  E  U
R  S  O  R  B  O  L  O  U  G  A  D
U  C  I  L  L  A  U  T  C  N  U  P
C  A  E  V  P  S  E  H  T  Y  C  S
T  N  E  S  E  R  P  E  R  S  I  M
```

EVOLVE	HEARTILY	SPECTATOR
NAUSEA	IRRITANT	CONDESCEND
NEURAL	PALATIAL	RECONSTRUCT
SCYTHE	PRISTINE	SUGGESTIBLE
DUCTILE	PUNCTUAL	COMMISSARIAT
NURTURE	IRRITABLE	MISREPRESENT

solution: _ _ _ _ _ _ _ _ _ _ _ _ _ _

82. FISH

```
S  A  R  G  A  S  S  U  M  F  I  S  H  R  K
S  S  A  B  E  T  A  R  E  P  M  E  T  C  U
S  S  A  B  H  T  U  O  M  E  G  R  A  L  G
C  H  U  B  S  U  C  K  E  R  I  J  A  O  N
G  R  S  A  W  S  H  A  R  K  W  W  R  A  I
I  N  S  M  O  O  T  H  T  O  N  G  U  E  T
L  I  A  T  G  A  L  F  L  A  H  S  I  L  I
D  E  R  E  D  V  E  L  V  E  T  F  I  S  H
P  J  A  P  A  N  E  S  E  E  E  L  E  R  W
H  T  U  O  M  Y  R  W  C  Y  G  R  O  P  H
```

BURI	WRYMOUTH	SMOOTHTONGUE
WALU	SAW SHARK	RED VELVETFISH
PORGY	CHUBSUCKER	SARGASSUM FISH
ILISHA	YELLOW BASS	TEMPERATE BASS
WHITING	YELLOW JACK	LARGEMOUTH BASS
FLAGTAIL	JAPANESE EEL	

solution: _ _ _   _ _ _ _ _ _   _ _ _ _ _

83. SPORTS

```
W S C I T S A N M Y G W R R E
C O T S P T P G L T C E I S N
R L R R G A N O L H T A C E D
O O G H O I I U G T L O N M G
S P O R T K A N I O R O R O E
S C J F O V E H T E S R S H E
B B A T T I N G O B A T T E R
O R R O L L E R S K A T I N G
W A T E R S K I I N G L M C A
B U N T E T H E R B A L L N K
```

JOG	THROW	DECATHLON
BUNT	VAULT	PAINTBALL
HOME	BATTER	GYMNASTICS
LOSE	HITTER	POGO STICK
POLO	STROKE	TETHERBALL
CANOE	BATTING	WATERSKIING
SCORE	RAFTING	ROLLER SKATING
SPORT	CROSSBOW	

solution: _ _ _ _ _ _ _ _ _   _ _ _ _ _ - _ _ _ _ _

84. ANIMALS

```
W F F I T S A M L L U B
E K A N S W A N A U G I
H D O P L A H P E C N I
E K A L T A D E L T A T
E F A L I A U Q T C T W
N O T K N A L P O O Z E
D G I P A E N I U G A C
A P U K R A H S E A L D
O R T H A C A N T H U S
C H I N Y Y A J E U L B
```

RAY	QUAIL	GUINEA PIG
YAK	SHARK	EKALTADELTA
GNAT	SNAIL	ZOOPLANKTON
SEAL	SNAKE	BULL MASTIFF
SWAN	IGUANA	ORTHACANTHUS
TOAD	BLUE JAY	
MACAW	CEPHALPOD	

solution: _ _ _ _ _   _ _ _ _ _   _ _ _ _ _ _ _ _

85. CARS

```
I L N C M A S E R A T I
Y A M A H A M I N I H Y
I N I H G R O B M A L R
A D A L N T Y I N S Y O
N R E S R M T S M E O S
E O U R S S A U L D H N
S V T C U I E T R E C A
N E C O A F N O R C R M
E R K A R E F L N A O I
J A C A B P O R S C H E
```

NSU	LOTUS	MANSORY
RUF	MATRA	PORSCHE
FORD	JENSEN	CHRYSLER
LADA	NISSAN	MASERATI
MINI	PROTON	MITSUOKA
ACURA	SIMSON	LAND ROVER
HANSA	YAMAHA	LAMBORGHINI
HORCH	BENTLEY	

solution: _ _ _ _ _ _ _ _ _ _ _ _ _ _ _ _

86. DOGS

```
S U S S E X S P A N I E L W E
S T A H I R E I R R E T T A R
R A L S Z I V I G E H L A U N
E B U L L D O G S D X W H H I
I T K E T Z R E T N I O P A G
R E I R R E T N O T S O B U E
R R R O P L O T T I L U P H I
A E B J A P A N E S E C H I N
H S A M O Y E D T E P P I H W
G R E A T P Y R E N E E S C R
```

PUG	BULLDOG	RAT TERRIER
PULI	HARRIER	JAPANESE CHIN
BOXER	MALTESE	BOSTON TERRIER
PLOTT	POINTER	GREAT PYRENEES
BORZOI	SAMOYED	SUSSEX SPANIEL
SALUKI	WHIPPET	
VIZSLA	CHIHUAHUA	

solution: _ _ _ _ _ _ _ _ _ _ _ _ _ _ _ _ _ _ _ _ _ _ _ _

87. TOUGH WORDS

```
I S D L I U B E R D U E
P N P I R T S T U O T T
C M A T S I V R E A R A
O O I C N S A A L N C L
A N N G C T A O P O T U
G O E N I E S T R I M G
U T C O U N S P I E D A
L O N S O B U S I S E O
A N N C A L I U I Q F C
N Y S C E I Q A D B U Y
T I M N E E F N L T L E
D E T A R O T C E P X E
```

ACME	REQUIEM	CORPULENT
PIQUE	DURATION	DISSATISFY
SINGE	MONOTONY	EXPECTORATE
VAPID	OUTSTRIP	DISCONSOLATE
VISTA	COAGULANT	INACCESSIBLE
FIASCO	COAGULATE	
REBUILD	CONNUBIAL	

solution: _ _ _ _ _ _ _ _ _ _ _ _ _ _

88. FISH

```
K L I A T D R O W S N E E R G
A D S M E L T W H I T I N G B
E L A B Y R I N T H F I S H E
J E L L Y N O S E F I S H R T
L I M A R U O G B A S S L E T
M A H S E E R E T R A D U P A
O M O S Q U I T O F I S H L R
R R A I N B O W T R O U T U P
A N O T U O R T A E S A G G S
A K T I G E R P E R C H O K I
```

IDE	SPRAT	MOSQUITOFISH
KOI	DARTER	RAINBOW TROUT
HOKI	GULPER	SMELT-WHITING
MORA	BASSLET	JELLYNOSE FISH
NASE	GOURAMI	LABYRINTH FISH
BETTA	MAHSEER	GREEN SWORDTAIL
CATLA	SEATROUT	
GRUNT	TIGERPERCH	

solution: _ _ _ _ _ _

89. FLOWERS

```
M R P A I T E U Q U O B
A U R R A A Z Y B K I E
G P I E S I A M L T T P
N S H T N R O E T L R O
O K E N R C R E A I E P
L R I O S U R N M O L P
I A W K A R T R M I C Y
A L C L O A O S T O C K
O O N O N S O P A N S Y
C I T A E C P E O N Y A
```

IRIS	STOCK	LARKSPUR
ASTER	LAUREL	MAGNOLIA
COSMO	YARROW	PRIMROSE
PANSY	ZINNIA	COCKSCOMB
PEONY	BOUQUET	BITTERROOT
POPPY	LANTANA	NASTURTIUM

solution: _ _ _ _ _ _ _ _ _ _ _ _ _ _ _ _ _ _ _

90. FRUITS

```
W H O R T L E B E R R Y
A B A G N A M S M C N A
X B O Y S E N B E R R Y
G U L E V B E R O L N T
O L O I B C I H E A O O
U A L F A M T L C C F T
R O T F A W I E I Y A A
D M G N A S P R A M L R
R I I H N D P L E A B A
P R A E P A R G A E S I
```

BAEL	LYCHEE	PIGFACE
IMBE	TOTARA	HAWTHORN
PEAR	APRICOT	SEA GRAPE
OLIVE	BILIMBI	WAX GOURD
PECAN	CERIMAN	BOYSENBERRY
SAFOU	MANGABA	WHORTLEBERRY

solution: _ _ _ _ _ - _ _ _ _ _ _ _ _ _ _ _

91. MATH

```
P Y E E R G E D R F N T
F I F T E E N O R E Z H
N A H T R E T A E R G T
H T A M T C C T F N H T
C R A B A T X G I O S H
O O U F A I R T U R U I
S S E L S A N S S B R R
I T S E Q U A L H E O T
N O R C O N S T A N T Y
E E M C D I V I S I O N
```

ORB	TORUS	SUBTEND
FOUR	COSINE	CONSTANT
LESS	DEGREE	COUNTING
MATH	FACTOR	DIVISION
RATE	THIRTY	FRACTALS
ZERO	FIFTEEN	THOUSAND
EQUAL	SIXTEEN	GREATER THAN

solution: _ _ _ _ _ _ _ _ _ _ ' _ _ _ _ _ _ _

92. SNAKES

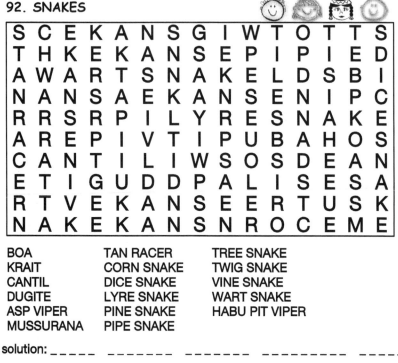

```
S C E K A N S G I W T O T T S
T H K E K A N S E P I P I E D
A W A R T S N A K E L D S B I
N A N S A E K A N S E N I P C
R R S R P I L Y R E S N A K E
A R E P I V T I P U B A H O S
C A N T I L I W S O S D E A N
E T I G U D D P A L I S E S A
R T V E K A N S E E R T U S K
N A K E K A N S N R O C E M E
```

BOA	TAN RACER	TREE SNAKE
KRAIT	CORN SNAKE	TWIG SNAKE
CANTIL	DICE SNAKE	VINE SNAKE
DUGITE	LYRE SNAKE	WART SNAKE
ASP VIPER	PINE SNAKE	HABU PIT VIPER
MUSSURANA	PIPE SNAKE	

solution: _ _ _ _ _   _ _ _ _ _ _ _   _ _ _ _ _ _ _   _ _ _ _ _ _ _ _ _   _ _ _ _ _

93. NUMBER SEARCH

```
5 6 5 8 5 6 4 7 2 3 8 0 2 4 0
3 5 9 9 8 0 3 3 1 5 4 6 2 4 0
7 0 0 6 7 8 3 6 6 5 2 0 4 4 2
0 0 4 6 6 0 8 7 3 9 2 2 4 2 1
9 1 2 2 5 7 9 5 6 1 0 9 2 4 6
9 8 9 9 5 3 2 5 5 3 9 3 7 7 5
5 9 3 4 5 0 8 2 8 5 1 4 7 4 8
7 0 3 6 0 3 3 5 7 7 7 6 7 8 5
4 2 8 1 6 0 5 7 9 5 0 6 0 3 3
9 9 1 6 6 4 9 0 6 2 2 4 5 7 7
```

4338928	5658564	9810056	35856120
1546240	7392242	39355235	1649266
0293466	21636587	18339240	7753306
7836652	24427770	0165975	6094661
37099574	33089953	7754226	1582805
6057950	73847424	0420832	

94. KIDS' WORDS

```
T R I K S M E G E B R T
R E E C I U J C O A E Y
G N E T H P N L I L O H
B I L O H I T I E L D O
A A G R G G L V M I O S
D R A C G N I D A R T P
M T E O R S I F U O E I
I S D K I Y C M E G G T
N A I O A O I B A R N A
T O N X L B U N E L I L
O R E D I L S E G D F F
N S A I L I N G S H I P
```

PIG	EAGLE	FLAMINGO
SIX	GREEN	HOSPITAL
BOLT	JUICE	STRAINER
BULL	ROAST	TERMINUS
COLD	SKIRT	BADMINTON
DOLL	SLIDE	TELEVISION
GOLD	CRYING	FIREFIGHTER
BAKER	POLICE	SAILING SHIP
CHILD	GORILLA	TRADING CARD

solution: _ _ _ _ _ - _ _ - _ _ _ _ _

95. KIDS' WORDS

```
H M A I L B O X I E D T
E S A M B U L A N C E C
W A C T Y B T O B K A N
W O N H H R M R R M D U
Y O L E O E E A E A O M
D E L L V O M L L R B
P I L L A R L A T E U E
T E E L E W S C T U C R
Y W E P U Y S L H I C Y
T T U L I P E S M I C K
E S E K O H C O M B L S
A T L A S M C Y S I A D
```

ONE   DAISY   MAILBOX
SKY   RULER   SHELTER
BOMB   SALAD   SWALLOW
COMB   TULIP   TROLLEY
LAMB   NUMBER   AMBULANCE
MOLE   PILLAR   MATHEMATICS
TILE   PULLEY   SCHOOLCHILD
ATLAS   TWELVE   SUPERMARKET
CAMEL   YELLOW
COMIC   CUTLERY

solution: _ _ _ _ - _ _ _ - _ _ _ _

96. VOCABULARY

```
I H V L U A H A U N T E
C N O Y S S O L G N X T
O R C S N U S V E C G N
E U A A P O P N E E E A
R T T Z N I I P R L A T
A I I U R T T I U I F T
M C O R R I A A L T F E
T A N E O T L T B A L L
H T P N R C I S I L U I
G M A I V I T A L O E D
I L C A T F Y I O V N N
N S G L U T L U M U T E
```

BLUR   TUMULT   GERIATRICS
GLUT   AFFLUENT   HOSPITABLE
HAUL   TACITURN   EXCEPTIONAL
MUTE   VOCATION   HOSPITALITY
AZURE   VOLATILE   IMPERTINENT
HAUNT   NIGHTMARE   INCANTATION
VITAL   DILETTANTE
GLOSSY   FICTITIOUS

solution: _ _ _ _ _ _ _ _ _ _ _ _

97. KIDS' WORDS

```
P P T P C O A T R A C K
B E E T L E I L C M N R
S A D D L E A A U G S A
R C D N E D L S I C T P
C E Y D E E I S A T L R
I G B M N C D I O O A A
N A E D I A N O B O S C
E P A L O A B A B N H I
M R R R E I N D L G T R
A A U C K A L A N A A E
G S O S N I B I M I B M
H E X A W F R O G E W A
```

BIN	BANANA	CALENDAR
MAN	BEETLE	CAR PARK
FROG	CINEMA	SKI BOOT
GAME	GARLIC	COAT RACK
PAGE	RUSH	ROAD SIGN
PEAR	SADDLE	WILD BOAR
RING	AMERICA	WIND BAND
AXE	BALANCE	BATH SALTS
MEDAL	MUSIC	TEDDY BEAR
PEACE	OCEANIA	

solution: _ _ _ _ _ _ _ _

98. KIDS' WORDS

```
P  I  T  R  O  U  S  E  R  S  W  O  R  L  D
N  E  W  Y  E  A  R  S  D  A  Y  G  A  R  M
P  B  P  T  E  L  E  T  T  E  R  N  N  D  G
A  M  C  I  E  E  L  C  O  N  T  I  O  N  N
N  U  F  C  P  L  H  O  F  E  A  N  I  A  I
T  H  G  I  L  T  E  E  R  T  S  T  T  S  T
I  T  L  U  O  R  S  N  N  T  N  H  A  U  A
E  Z  U  W  S  U  D  U  U  I  N  G  T  O  K
S  E  E  U  O  T  O  A  A  M  F  I  S  H  S
R  R  T  H  N  M  I  P  T  H  T  L  A  T  U
K  O  O  B  E  S  I  C  R  E  X  E  U  P  B
L  H  A  N  D  K  E  R  C  H  I  E  F  R  E
```

ARM	AUGUST	TROUSERS
BUS	LETTER	LIGHTNING
CITY	MITTEN	WATCHTOWER
DATE	TURTLE	STREETLIGHT
FISH	LANTERN	EXHAUST PIPE
GLUE	PANTIES	HANDKERCHIEF
ZERO	SKATING	PAINT ROLLER
HOUSE	STATION	EXERCISE BOOK
LOTUS	MOUNTAIN	NEW YEAR'S DAY
THUMB	PAINTING	
WORLD	THOUSAND	

solution: _ _ _ _ _   _ _   _ _ _ _ _ _ _ _ _

99. KIDS' WORDS

```
W F R A W D R U M S T I C K P
G R E S S E R D R I A H R C O
H R S N W E A R T H O A U A M
T E O E E F T H A R P A M J E
I S R T R W U A S T T H B R G
M C E U T R S E K K I P A E R
S C I S S O R S C S I U P B A
D T O D G A B R T U E T G M N
L P A E C U E O R A T C T U A
O Y Y I S T R R L E N T I L T
G O N H A Y B D T A S D E K E
T G Z W E T X O B R E W O L F
```

TOY   EARTH   HISTORY   ICE SKATE
BUSH   FRUIT   LETTUCE   NEWSSTAND
DRUG   SCREW   SKITTLE   FLOWER BOX
PARK   WATER   SCISSORS   LUMBERJACK
POST   GROTTO   THURSDAY   HAIRDRESSER
ROSE   GUITAR   TREASURE   POMEGRANATE
ZOO   LENTIL   DRUMSTICK   HORSE-RACING
CRUMB   DWARF   GOLDSMITH

solution: _ _ _ _ _ _ _ _ _ _   _ _ _ _ _ _

- 58 -

100. KIDS' WORDS

```
H N O R G A N I M A L S
T I A Y L L E B B O L G
O E P C T E O L U E O N
Y P A P G W A D E O Y I
S O C H O N S P D C M L
O L E R K P I M R O M K
L E C E E N O R N M U C
D V T A G R I T E E D U
I N K B N N H P A T S D
E E A I I T I W O M A N
R G N D N N E K S K U W
O G A L E P I H C R A S
```

ANT	COMET	ENVELOPE
BOW	DUMMY	ARCHIPELAGO
CROW	MONTH	LOUDSPEAKER
KING	ORGAN	TOY SOLDIER
NINE	WOMAN	GOOD MORNING
PINE	ANIMAL	HIPPOPOTAMUS
PINK	BLANKET	SLEEPING BAG
BELLY	DUCKLING	WATERING CAN

solution: _ _ _ _ _ _ _ ' _ _ _ _ _

101. KIDS' WORDS

```
R E T S I S R A L U C O N I B
D S S A K W S I M S H O W E R
C R R N M R Y I L I G D L T A
O N A D O T O E L Y K C O G V
M P G W X W E W L V Y W F W E
P Z U I I P M O E C E A A C N
U I S C Y N P A I R Y R W H E
T G Z H O S G R N S I C N N V
E Z E Z A U T U M N Y F I V E
R A T N A R U A T S E R T N S
D G O O D E V E N I N G U J U
U M E S K I P P I N G R O P E
```

CUP	SUGAR	COMPUTER
JUG	SYRUP	SANDWICH
DOWN	TOWER	TRICYCLE
FAWN	AUTUMN	UNICYCLE
FIVE	SHOWER	FIREWORKS
HAWK	SILVER	BINOCULARS
YAWN	SISTER	RESTAURANT
PIZZA	ZIGZAG	SLEEPYHEAD
RAVEN	DRAWING	GOOD EVENING
SEVEN	POLYGON	SKIPPING ROPE
SIXTY	SNOWMAN	

solution: _ _ _ _ _ _ _ _   _ _ _ _ _ _ _

102. SUDOKU

	5			4	
		6	3		
2					6
1					2
		4	1		
	3			5	

103. ODD-EVEN

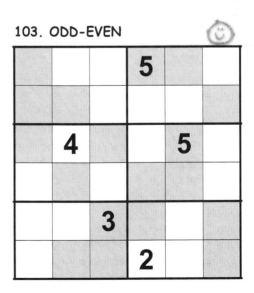

			5		
	4			5	
		3			
			2		

104. DIAGONAL

	2			6	
	6			4	
1					4
6					3
	1			3	
	5			1	

105. CALCUDOKU

7+	12+		150×	4-	
					2-
15+		3÷	2-	6×	
					11+
1-	17+		10+		
		5÷			

106. HIDOKU

2			44			48
1	3	41	12	11	46	49
20		5	40			9
	21		6			31
	22		15	7	32	
23	17	16	37		29	
	25			28		34

1.

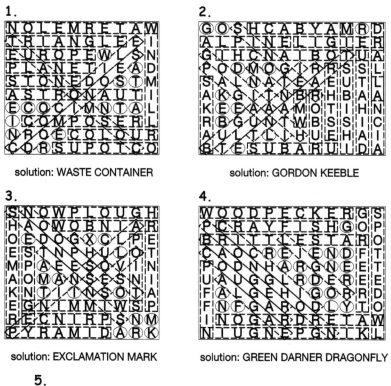

solution: WASTE CONTAINER

2.

solution: GORDON KEEBLE

3.

solution: EXCLAMATION MARK

4.

solution: GREEN DARNER DRAGONFLY

5.

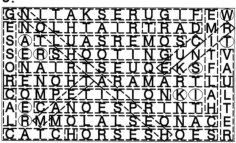

solution: WATERSKIER

6.

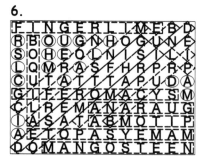

solution: ROUGH SHELL MACADAMIA

7.

solution: MERRY CHRISTMAS

8.

solution: STICKING PLASTER

9.

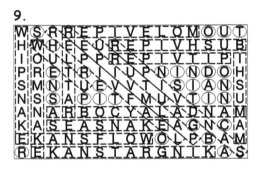

solution: SOUTHERN INDONESIAN SPITTING COBRA

10.

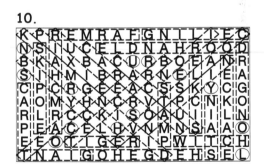

solution: NURSERY SCHOOL

11.

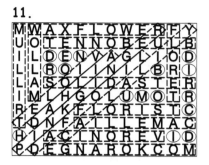

solution: DENDROBIUM ORCHID

12.

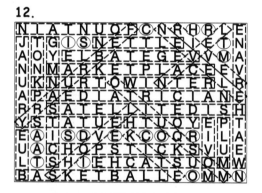

solution: CHRISTMAS DECORATION

13.

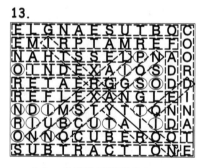

solution: POISSON DISTRIBUTION

14.

solution: MEDICINE CABINET

15.

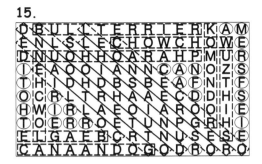

solution: AMERICAN STAFFORDSHIRE TERRIER

16.

solution: SCHOOL CARETAKER

17.

solution: CALIFORNIA SPANGLED CAT

18.

solution: FATHER CHRISTMAS

19.

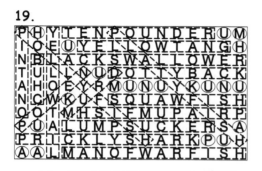

solution: HUMUHUMU-NUKUNUKU-APUA'A

20.

solution: WASHING MACHINE

21.

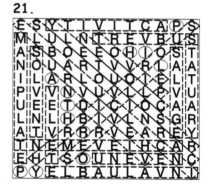

solution: PHILANTHROPY

22.

solution: TABLE TENNIS BAT

23.

solution: PHALAENOPSIS ORCHID

24.

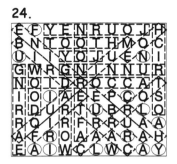

solution: FUNICULAR RAILWAY

25.

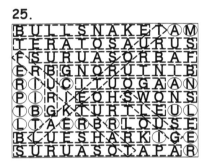

solution: AMERICAN PIT BULL TERRIER

26.

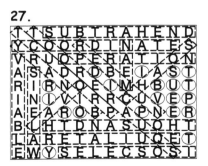

solution: FARM WORKER

27.

solution: DISTRIBUTIVE PROPERTY

28.

solution: CONTEMPORANEOUS

29.

solution: SPINY MONKEY-ORANGE

30.

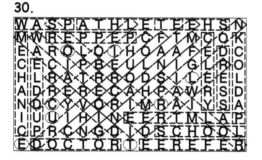

solution: OIL CRUET

31.

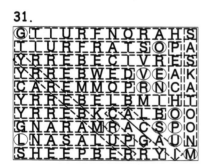

solution: GOVERNOR'S PLUM

32.

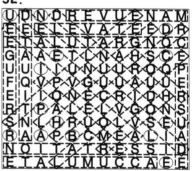

solution: UNDECIPHERABLE

33.

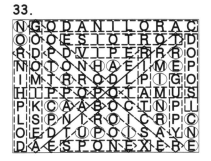

solution: NORTH AMERICAN PORCUPINE

34.

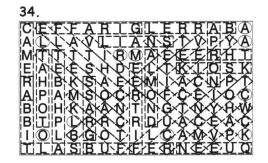

solution: ALARM CLOCK

35.

solution: AMERICAN RED RASPBERRY

36.

solution: SHIP'S WHEEL

37.

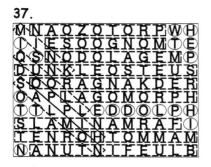

solution: WHITE-SPOTTED DOLPHIN

38.

solution: MERCEDES-BENZ

39.

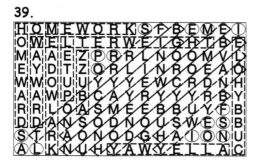

solution: SEMIPROFESSIONAL

40.

solution: SLIMY SCULPIN

41.

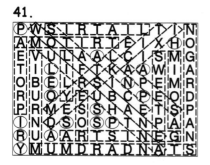

solution: PHALAENOPSIS SPRAY

42.

solution: PRIME MERIDIAN

43.

solution: ENJOY YOUR TRIP

44.

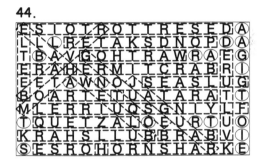

solution: ALDABRA GIANT TORTOISE

45.

solution: QUESTION MARK

46.

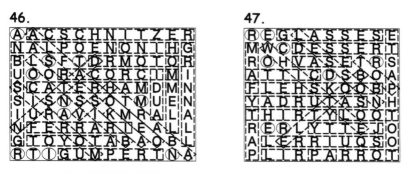

solution: ASTON MARTIN

47.

solution: RECORDER

48.

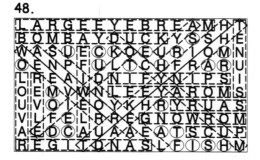

solution: SUCKERMOUTH ARMORED CATFISH

49.

solution: SEWING MACHINE

50.

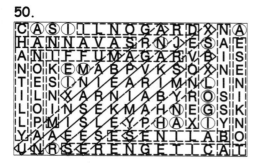

solution: ASIAN SEMI-LONGHAIR

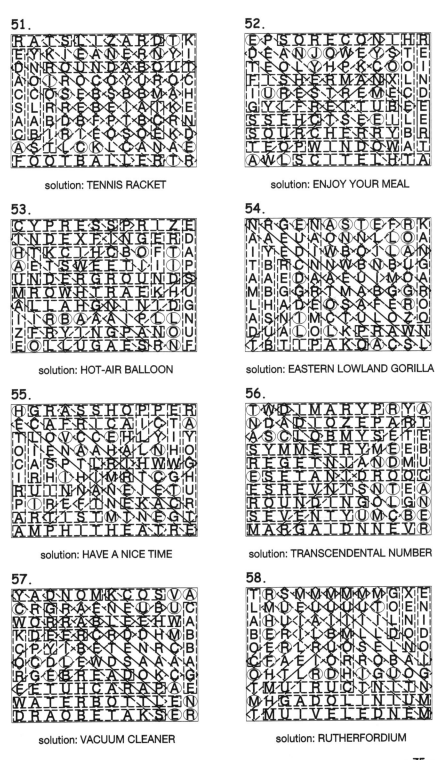

51.

solution: TENNIS RACKET

52.

solution: ENJOY YOUR MEAL

53.

solution: HOT-AIR BALLOON

54.

solution: EASTERN LOWLAND GORILLA

55.

solution: HAVE A NICE TIME

56.

solution: TRANSCENDENTAL NUMBER

57.

solution: VACUUM CLEANER

58.

solution: RUTHERFORDIUM

59.

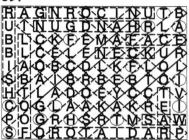

solution: TRAFFIC LIGHTS

60.

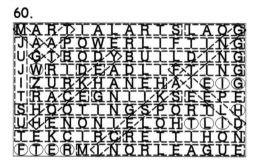

solution: WEIGHTLIFTER

61.

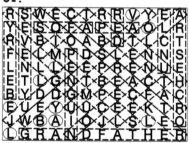

solution: VOLLEYBALL

62.

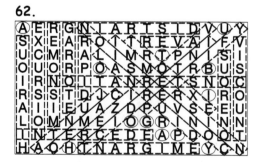

solution: AUTOBIOGRAPHY

63.

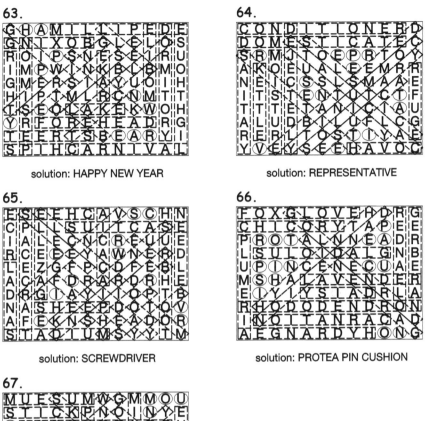

solution: HAPPY NEW YEAR

64.

solution: REPRESENTATIVE

65.

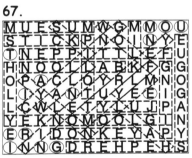

solution: SCREWDRIVER

66.

solution: PROTEA PIN CUSHION

67.

solution: MOUNTAINEERING

68.

solution: SIAMESE FIGHTING FISH

69.

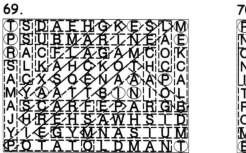

solution: TEMPERA PAINT

70.

solution: PINK-FLOWERED NATIVE RASPBERRY

71.

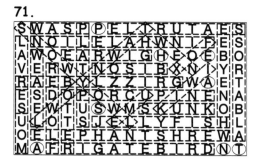

solution: PHEASANT

72.

solution: CONSTELLATION

73.

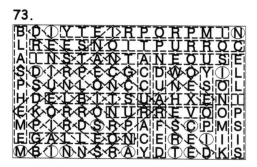

solution: INDISCRIMINATE

74.

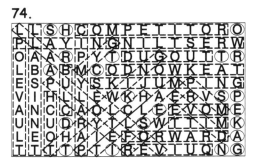

solution: SHORT TRACK SPEED SKATING

75.

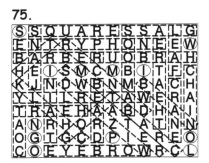

solution: SWIMMING POOL

76.

solution: DEGREE OF AN ANGLE

77.

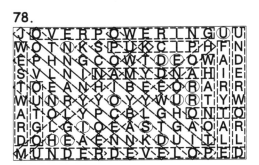

solution: FLAG FOOTBALL

78.

solution: UNDERNOURISHED

79.

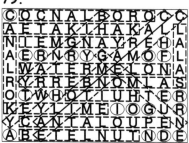

solution: CHERRY OF THE RIO GRANDE

80.

solution: ZEBRA LONGWING BUTTERFLY

81.

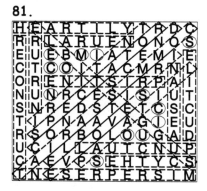

solution: SEMICONSCIOUS

82.

solution: RIO GRANDE PERCH

83.

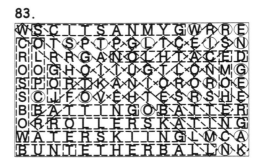

solution: WRESTLING GRECO-ROMAN

84.

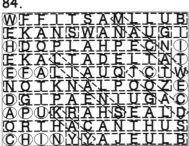

solution: WHITE FACED CAPUCHIN

85.

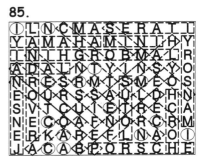

solution: INTERMECCANICA

86.

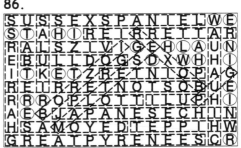

solution: WEST HIGHLAND WHITE TERRIER

87.

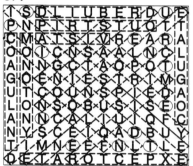

solution: SUPERINTENDENT

88.

solution: KALUGA

89.

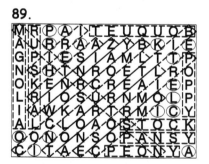

solution: PARAKEET HELICONIA

90.

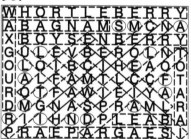

solution: SMALL-LEAF TAMARIND

91.

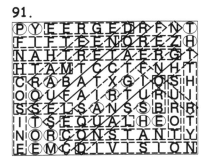

solution: PYTHAGORAS' THEOREM

92.

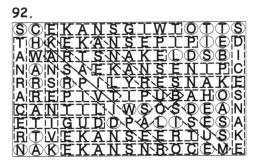

solution: SCOTT SHIELDS BARROWS DEADLIEST SNAKE

93.

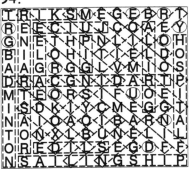

94.

solution: MERRY-GO-ROUND

95.

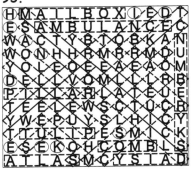

solution: HIDE-AND-SEEK

96.

solution: CONVERSATION

97.

solution: PINE CONE

98.

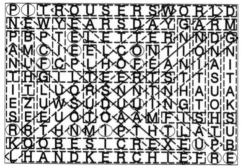

solution: PIECE OF FURNITURE

99.

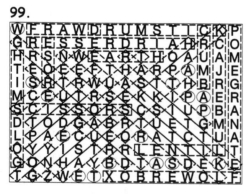

solution: WASTEPAPER BASKET

100.

solution: TEACHER'S DESK

101.

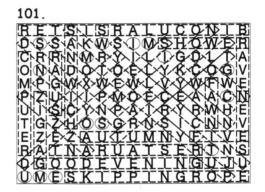

solution: SWIMMING COSTUME

102.

3	5	2	6	4	1
4	1	6	3	2	5
2	4	3	5	1	6
1	6	5	4	3	2
5	2	4	1	6	3
6	3	1	2	5	4

103.

1	2	4	5	3	6
5	3	6	4	2	1
3	4	1	6	5	2
6	5	2	3	1	4
2	6	3	1	4	5
4	1	5	2	6	3

104.

4	2	1	3	6	5
5	6	3	2	4	1
1	3	5	6	2	4
6	4	2	1	5	3
2	1	4	5	3	6
3	5	6	4	1	2

105.

3	1	4	5	2	6
4	3	2	6	5	1
5	2	1	4	6	3
6	4	3	2	1	5
1	5	6	3	4	2
2	6	5	1	3	4

106.

2	42	43	44	45	47	48
(1)	3	41	12	11	46	(49)
20	4	5	40	13	10	9
19	21	39	6	14	8	31
18	22	38	15	7	32	30
23	17	16	37	36	29	33
24	25	26	27	28	35	34

Made in the USA
Lexington, KY
22 November 2015